D.O.M.

D.O.M.
Rediscovering Brazilian Ingredients
Alex Atala

Φ

Contents

Foreword – Alain Ducasse

The first scene took place in Brazil at the start of 2011. I was visiting São Paulo and, as is my wont, devoting large chunks of time to immersing myself in the atmospheric surroundings of the vibrant city. A friend of mine who lives in the city said to me: 'There is a young Brazilian chef that you absolutely have to meet.' You guessed it – that young chef was Alex Atala. So off I went to the magnificent Jardins district of the city. It was still early when I arrived at D.O.M., and Alex suggested that we went to a market... my favourite hobby. The trip was revelatory. Everywhere there were local ingredients, and I found myself smelling, feeling and chewing the remarkable produce on display at every opportunity. The other revelation was Alex's understanding of these ingredients – an intimacy bordering on fervent passion. Going to a market with him is like diving into the very depths of the Brazilian land.

Scene two took place a few hours later in his restaurant on Rua Barão de Capanema. There the magic continued. With each mouthful of his food it was clear that Alex knew how to channel all of his knowledge of these ingredients, and the emotion he felt for them, into his cooking. What ought to have been just a lunch resonated for much longer: we spoke, we ate... it was nothing short of momentous.

The third scene took place in my native France. For a long time I had wanted to gather together various chefs that I had met from all over the world in Paris to introduce them to the food aficionados over here, believing that by reaching out and learning from the remarkable food being produced around the world that we could further our own cooking and drive forward gastronomy as a whole. So it was that in January 2012 I organised the first of my essential meetings, and I invited Alex Atala to devise the very first menu. We had his famous priprioca, of course, as well as black rice, mandioquinha, taperabá and brazil nuts. And then the manioc root in its many different incarnations: tapioca, chibé, tucupi... The guests, captivated by the remarkable ingredients and skilfull preparations, fell under his spell just as I had six months earlier in São Paulo.

There are, of course, two obvious factors that explain Alex's success: work and talent. Work in the form of the long initiation process carried out in Europe. He first arrived in Belgium, then moved to France, and finally ended up in Italy. Over the course of these wanderings he has passed through some very fine kitchens, including those of Jean-Pierre Bruneau in Brussels and Bernard Loiseau in Saulieu. As for talent, what follows in this book shows that he has no shortage in that department.

But there is also another explanation. A phenomenon that is separate from Alex and is to do with contemporary cooking. To do with the powerful dynamic that is lighting the way for Alex's success, and which makes the book in your hands all the more important.

Let's go back to the start. The young Brazilian, barely 20 years old, discovers cooking in Europe. He learns classical techniques, particularly French techniques. He becomes aware of the fact that in contemporary French cooking, techniques are considered secondary to ingredients. When he returns to Brazil at the start of the 1990s, he looks around him: where are the ingredients to which I am going to apply these new techniques? They exist, of course. But they are far away – not just in geographic terms, but also psychologically. These are simple ingredients used by humble people, a far cry from the urbane, accepted practices from the world of international cuisine. So Alex embarks on a quest. To redefine traditional Brazilian ingredients and local understanding by incorporating them into the best modern and classical cooking techniques.

This movement of chefs seeking to redefine the importance of land and place is, in my mind, the most important phenomenon taking place today in the world of gastronomy. We see it in Brazil – Alex has been one of its pioneering figures. We also see it in many other countries, with each chef taking advantage of his country's own unique larder.

It is an irresistible force. It is in the process of profoundly reshaping the landscape of world cooking – skill and knowledge are nowadays truly shared, and talent can be found everywhere. As a result, every single country can, potentially, play out their role in the great global theatre of gastronomy.

This also spells a wonderful celebration of the vitality of cooking. Using the same basic techniques (essentially French ones, as it happens), each one, within its own context and culture, is equal to the task of identifying, renewing and reviving its culinary tradition. In the presence of such a proliferation, everyone is a winner.

This is a positive movement for the planet, too. When cooks look for produce that is available around them, they come face to face with producers. Even better, they begin to show concern for the way in which this produce is grown or gathered, for how our seas are fished. Preference goes to those responsible producers who work in balance with nature – after all it is they who produce the best, most delicious ingredients. The result is an exemplary link between the producer and the chef, one which has the capacity to bring about a real transformation in the care we take when managing rare resources. This is especially important in Brazil, a country whose unique natural resources and remarkable environment are under constant threat.

In this fine and appetising book, Alex Atala bears witness to his vision of tomorrow's cuisine. This is his manifesto for food that is local, healthy, fair and seasonal, and which respects ingredients, sustainability and the environment.

Enjoy the feast!

Introduction

When I started my restaurant, D.O.M., in 1999 I simply needed to make some money and had no great ambitions. Before I even started thinking about refined cuisine, about searching for new ingredients and exploring the other concerns that I have today, D.O.M. had to be viable as a business. And to run a restaurant in a large city such as São Paulo is a highly complex, and highly competitive, activity.

Let's go back in time. I started cooking during a classic backpacking trip around Europe. I had the honour and the pleasure to work in Belgium, France and Italy, and from each of those places I brought a souvenir, a lesson learned, a message, which are all present in my work to this day. Among those messages, the one that speaks clearest is the one that I shall never cook Belgian cuisine as a Belgian chef will, nor French food as a French chef nor Italian food as an Italian chef. There's a very simple reason. Even if I am able to execute the recipes, those flavours are not part of my cultural register. My cultural register is Brazilian. At some point in my journey I also understood that none of them could cook Brazilian food as well as I could. Its wild flavours have been part of my life since childhood – infancy, even. My father and my grandfather were fishermen and hunters. To walk in the rainforest, to explore unknown, undervalued flavours, are things that I have done for ever.

When I came back to Brazil in 1994, by now a professional chef, I did not have enough money to open my own restaurant, so I went to work for others. When you are a hired chef you work to a brief, to a philosophy conceived by others. At the request of my employers, I prepared the Italian, French and Belgian recipes that were part of my baggage. Because I am impertinent, I slowly started offering my own variations on the dishes. Foreign chefs who worked in Brazil at that time had already started using Brazilian ingredients to prepare classic recipes. I took the risk of following them down that path. These small interventions were successful and raised my confidence. Years passed, and I finally had the opportunity to open my own restaurant. But there was a difficult choice to make: which style would I adopt?

I hope that people will not be too surprised to learn that D.O.M. was not born a gastronomic restaurant. With practice, it evolved and clearly started to assume the identity of a Brazilian restaurant. In the dining room, the restaurant is as Brazilian as possible. From the hand soap used in the restrooms – made in Brazil, from brazil nuts – to the chairs, known as Oscar chairs, an hommage by the designer Sérgio Rodrigues to the architect Oscar Niemeyer, everything exudes Brazil. Even the sculptures in the kitchen were made by Conceição do Bugres, a popular artist from the Mato Grosso region. Our service, too, is Brazilian in style: attentive and quiet, but also cordial and kind. There is an eagerness to please, which is innately Brazilian. A restaurant's staff can be enchanting if well trained. At D.O.M., we strive to achieve this kind of quality.

The need to search for national ingredients kept beating inside my chest. Whenever possible, at weekends I went fishing or into the rainforest, and I always came back with something – a new kind of herb, a fruit, a fish. But in a city of 19 million people, it was impossible to go out and forage in this way and to come back the same day to make lunch or dinner. I began to understand that my relationship with Brazilian ingredients needed to be restructured.

Similarly, my attitude to technique had to be readdressed. As happens with all passions, there was a stage when technique was very important at D.O.M.. The dishes we prepared were once more complex. But over time I realized that the main message that I wanted to impart, which was about the flavour of Brazilian ingredients at their best, sometimes got lost.

The essence of Brazilian cuisine is very simple – which does not mean it is easy. Brazilian ingredients are in vogue. Technique became a tool to bring out the best from each ingredient, playing a secondary role in the recipes. I am still open to and enchanted by all techniques, both modern and classical, but I use them to get to a place I have not reached before. My cooking has pared itself down and switched its emphasis on to flavours, textures and ingredients.

As I talked to patrons in the dining room, I realized that Brazilian ingredients were finally gaining prominence. People had started to wake up to their existence. Today, I am sure my message is more accessible. The ingredients, and the best way to prepare them, are at the centre of conversations in the dining room. In this way, Brazilian ingredients go from force to force.

Another of my concerns is our relationship with the environment. This story is not always told. But it is about a chain that leads from grower or producer and ends up on the plate at the restaurant. The ties between urban people and forest people must be tightened. And cuisine has been an important tool for defending biodiversity.

Until very recently, the relationship between the consumer and nature was one of extraction. By using national ingredients at D.O.M., many of which had been forgotten until we revived them, we aim to enhance conservation and establish a new relationship between country and city. We defend a return to nature, and to achieve that end we must have the purest and least processed ingredients. This mission is far from simple, but it is an ideal that permeates our philosophy.

Let's talk now about ingredients that come from deep within Brazil. Many of the items that are listed in this book have not yet reached the aisles of my country's supermarkets. I dream about the day when this will happen, when unfamiliar ingredients start being used in our kitchens and thus gain in importance, relevance and usefulness. Through this search for, and use of, national ingredients I hope to assign value to my culture and nature as a whole. Forests must be more valuable while they are standing than when they are felled. And man has to be included in this context. Of course we must preserve rivers, seas and forests, but we must not forget another important element of this ecosystem: human beings. Conservation of nature must encompass all of these. And cuisine is able to forge a link between them.

A Short Story

I have been walking around the Amazon forest since I was a child, hunting, fishing and learning. Around the turn of the century I bought an area of land there. It was what we call a 'soft possession' – that is, it belonged to the Brazilian government but had been occupied for more than a hundred years by indigenous tribespeople. It may sound strange for someone who is not from Brazil, but this kind of thing still happens here. Part of the land was the subject of dispute, its ownership claimed by a native community which had nothing to do with the party who had sold it to me. Driven by good intentions, I went there; we talked and reached an agreement. As I believe that from conflict comes discussion, and from discussion comes solution, I was happy to give up part of what I had acquired and teach that community about the need to formalize their ownership of the land and, in return, pay taxes. Soon, peace began to reign over an area with a history of violent conflict. In a childish way I felt proud, victorious and benevolent.

Observing these people, I realized that there was no abject poverty, but that they did suffer from scarcity and malnutrition. So I decided to keep up my role as philanthropist and to send a 'staple foods basket' to all the families living there. A 'staple foods basket' is what we call the range of foodstuffs that an average Brazilian family consumes in a month; it includes rice, beans, cassava flour, coffee and sugar among other items.

When I went back to the area six months later I was appalled by the amount of litter. Plastic, cardboard boxes, cans and other packaging from the products that I had sent them were strewn all over the place. I gathered the community together and gave them the classic sustainability speech, saying that I had sent products to improve their lives and what I had got back was rubbish and degradation. Antonio, a short man, strong as a bull and very articulate, stood up and replied: 'Alex, it's your fault. For us, the packaging of a fruit is its skin, a fish's are its scales, an ox's is its hide, and these things can all be thrown on the ground. None of them are bad for the earth. You should not have sent us all these things wrapped in plastic.' I grew silent as I realized that playing God is not simple at all. I had thought I had something to teach them; in fact they had something to teach me. I should have known better: my own life experiences in the world and in the kitchen should have told me that.

Transformation Through Cooking
Cooking can be transformative, as evidenced by the lives of some of the best-known chefs of our day. Ferran Adriá began by washing dishes. René Redzepi started cooking because he was the son of immigrants. Geovane Carneiro, my sous-chef, came from Conceição do Coité, in Bahia. Although he has very little education, he does have one of the most refined palates that I have ever encountered. He does not make mistakes.

My path too was very unorthodox. Before becoming a chef I was a DJ, a punk boy, a creature of the night. I lived intensely and indulged in everything that our society tempts us with: rock 'n' roll, violence, drugs. Not all misfits will get the chance to become a world-renowned chef. But not all misfits are doomed. I think it is important to highlight in a book about a chef that there is more than one path to get here. The kitchen is pourous and sucks up all comers. Not only those who choose noble paths are accepted near the stove. And this is why the cooking profession has great potential for social change.

I am a guy who went into the kitchen thinking that I was in an orthodox world. I dressed as a cook and I covered my tattoos, my past. Today, thank God, I live in peace with who I am and who I was. I can broadcast a message of high cuisine, proud to be wacky. Even greater is the fact that cooking has enabled me to be a better citizen, to use the opportunities that this high visibility has granted me. In the following pages we will touch on matters cultural, economic, sociological, philosophical and environmental, because I believe that cuisine is the most important link between nature and culture.

Instituto ATA – ATA Institute

It all began with a passion; with the discovery of unique, undervalued and forgotten Brazilian ingredients; with the creation of recipes that could give these ingredients a function, so that they gained utility in the kitchen and, therefore, a higher demand in the market.

I believe in a fair, intelligent trade, based on a philosophy. But an extra step must be taken. It is not enough to pay for an ingredient. We must create levers to improve the way we use the sea, the rivers, the fields and forests. And we must not forget another important natural element, the human living in each of those regions.

It was with this in mind that I decided to ally myself to many experts from different areas and create an institute, ATA, in order to help structure chains of supply and seek ingredients for a type of cuisine that is not only pleasant to the taste, but also healthy for those who make it, for those who eat it and for those who produce it.
www.institutoata.org.br

Dairy and meat

Butters

Brazil is a tropical country, and the breed of cattle that has best adapted here is zebu (see page 44). Our meat and dairy products therefore taste slightly different from those of Europe and the United States. We have some tradition with dairy, and it is worth speaking a bit longer about some of it. Our butters have a high water content and, sometimes, low fat content. This gives them a special flavour and texture. For us Brazilians, these butters bring us back to our childhoods. They caramelize in a different way, they get golden in a different way, they have a different texture. This is where their ability to fascinate lies.

One of the most interesting butters in our culture is typical of the northeast and, legend says, was born from a process that went wrong. Some Portuguese colonizers tried to make cheeses similar to those they had eaten at home, *Azeitão* and *Serra da Estrela*. Since the raw materials, humidity and temperature were different, the process went wrong and the milk fat went rancid. This a poetic version of how *manteiga de garrafa*, or bottle butter, an important source of umami, the Japanese-style taste sensation, in our cuisine was born. In texture and flavour it is very close to the butter typically used in Indian cooking, known as ghee. On the other side of the world, through a different process but with the same milk from the same breed of cows, virtually identical products have emerged.

Chickpeas with Brazilian butter

SERVES 4

Ingredients

Chickpeas with Brazilian butter

- **150 g chickpeas, plus 12 extra for garnishing**
- **1 clove garlic**
- **40 g Brazilian butter (see page 26)**
- **onion coal**
- **salt and pepper**

Preparation

- Cook the chickpeas in boiling water until soft.
- Set aside 12 chickpeas for the garnish and mash the remainder with the garlic using a fork.
- Add the Brazilian butter, season with salt and pepper and stir to combine.

Finish and presentation

- Fry the remaining chickpeas in a little butter until golden and set aside.
- Divide the chickpea purée between 4 plates.
- Garnish each plate with 3 of the fried chickpeas and a sprinkling of onion coal.

Cheeses

In Brazil we have a tradition of making raw milk cheese, such as *queijo manteiga, queijo de coalho, queijo minas, queijo minas padrão* and the cheeses from the Canastra and Salitre mountains.

Among the cheeses made from cooked curd two stand out. One of them, *requeijão* – which, with its cream and brown variations, shows different flavours can be extracted from the same ingredient – is a real star. *Catupiry* is a cream cheese which has had starch added during processing and is very famous in Brazil. It was extremely popular from the 1960s to the 1980s but has since lost gastronomic ground, being stigmatized as dull and common. It was a cheap ingredient that ended up in the humblest kitchens.

In our towns and cities, there is a culture of consuming fried finger foods that can be eaten quickly. One of the icons of this culture is *coxinha*, which means 'little thigh' because it resembles a chicken thigh in shape. Its mass is usually made out of chicken stock mixed with potatoes or cassava and a little flour. This mixture is then filled with cooked chicken. Breaded and deep-fried, the *coxinha* has a spot in the heart of all Brazilians. The controversial *catupiry* is traditionally added. If you go to a small Brazilian bar and ask for a *coxinha*, they almost always ask whether you want it with or without *catupiry*. The addition of cheese makes the dish richer, creamier and more complex.

Black coxinha with catupiry

SERVES 4

	Ingredients	Preparation	Finish and presentation
Charred herbs	• **25 g rosemary** • **25 g mint** • **25 g coriander (cilantro)** • **25 g sweet chervil** • **25 g basil** • **25 g parsley** • **25 g thyme**	• Preheat the oven to 200°C/400°F. • Wrap the herbs in aluminium foil and place in the oven for 1 hour. • Raise the oven temperature to 250°C /480°F and cook for 30 minutes more. • Transfer the charred herbs to a Thermomix and beat to a fine powder. Pass through a sieve and set aside.	• **200 g catupiry (see page 30)** • **4 sprouts ora pro nobis, to garnish** • Put a generous spoonful of catupiry on each of 4 serving plates. • Place a coxinha in the centre if each plate. • Garnish with an *ora pro nobis* sprout.
Coxinha dough	• **500 ml chicken stock** • **500 g all purpose (plain) flour** • **salt**	• Heat the chicken stock in a pan and gradually add the flour, stirring continuously. • When the dough starts to come together, remove from the heat, season with salt and continue to beat until a firm dough is formed. Set aside.	
Coxinha filling	• **1 tbsp rapeseed (canola) oil** • **150 g red onion, brunoised** • **2 garlic cloves, finely chopped** • **250 g chicken breast, cooked and shredded** • **5 g spicy aromatic pepper** • **5 g colorau** • **10 g parsley** • **10 g coriander (cilantro)** • **salt**	• Heat the oil in a pan and fry the onion and garlic until soft. • Add the chicken, aromatic pepper and colorau and mix well. • Cook for several minutes more and add the parsley and the coriander (cilantro). Season with salt and set aside.	
Coxinha	• **coxinha dough (above)** • **coxinha filling (above)** • **150 ml milk** • **1 egg** • **charred herbs (above)** • **canola (rapeseed) oil, for deep frying**	• Roll the dough to a thickness of ½ in/1 cm. • Using a 10 cm/4 in ring cutter, cut 4 circles from the dough. • Place a generous spoonful of the filling into the centre of each circle of dough, bring up the edges to form a conical shape and seal by pressing the edges together at the tip. • Combine the milk with the egg. Roll each coxinha through this mixture and then through the charred herbs. • Deep-fry the coxinha in the rapeseed (canola) oil until crispy.	

Queijo de coalho

The most used cheese in Brazilian cuisine is called *queijo de coalho*. Its preparation is rustic. Milk at 35 degrees Celsius, curdling, wait for the reaction, drain the whey, put it into the tray. It can be consumed fresh, and, like this, it is called frescal. The most popular one is what we call meia cura, or half-cured, and is the next stage after frescal. With a skin already formed, it has a white middle and is quite salty. It is one of the ingredients used to make *pão de queijo*, or cheese buns, a Brazilian icon. From baião de dois to arroz de forno and so many other recipes, it is omnipresent in our culture, in our cuisine.

In my opinion, the most fun way to consume it is on the beach. Boys walk with a tin oven with some charcoals. They carry little trays with this cheese on the side. When you order one, the boys fan the charcoal and toast the cheese, which is often served with molasses.

In the Brazilian northeast, there is a variation of this cheese with more fat in it, and therefore a more elastic pulp. This cheese is called queijo manteiga, or butter cheese. Traditionally, it is used toasted on an iron skillet, and accompanies from breakfasts to tapioca. It is also an ingredient in a traditional North-eastern recipe: cartola, which consists of a slice of the cheese served with a roasted banana.

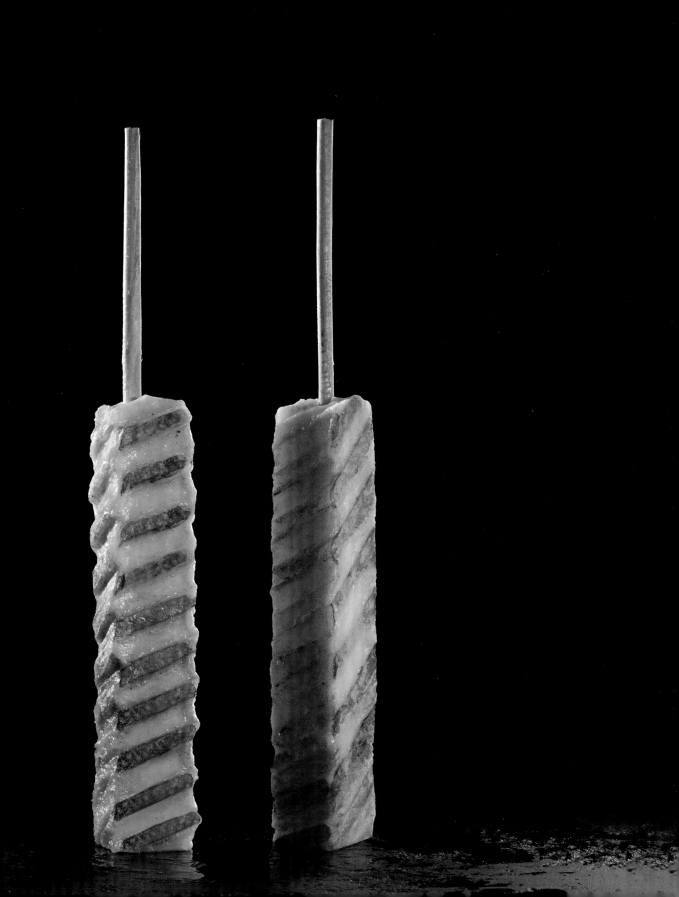

Manioc mille-feuilles

SERVES 4

Ingredients

Manioc mille-feuilles

• **2.3 kg manioc (see page 190), peeled**
• **500 g Brazilian butter (see page 26)**
• **300 g queijo de coalho (see page 34), grated**
• **4 tablespoons coarse salt**
• **salt**

Preparation

• Preheat the oven to 200°C/400°F.
• Using a mandoline, cut the manioc into 1 mm slices.
• Take a rectangular baking sheet as a base and start to construct the mille-feuille: Lay the first slice of manioc on the sheet and spread it with some of the Brazilian butter, then some of the *queijo de coalho* cheese.
• Lay the next slice of manioc directly over the first but crosswise, so that the top and bottom of this slice lie above the sides of the first slice.
• Press down firmly on the top layer using another baking sheet, so as to compress the layers tightly.
• Spread the second layer with more Brazilian butter and *queijo de coalho* cheese.
• Repeat the process, alternating the direction of each new layer, firmly compressing the layers each time before spreading the butter and cheese, until all the ingredients are used up and finishing with a slice of manioc.
• Cover the mille-feuille with aluminum foil and bake for 40 minutes.
• At the end of this time, remove from the oven and place a heavy weight on top, large enough to cover the entire surface area, in order to complete the compaction. When cold, set aside in the refrigerator for 6 hours.

Finish and presentation

• **500 ml Port wine**
• **150 g catupiry (see page 30)**
• **100 g chives, finely chopped**

• Place the Port wine in a medium pan and reduce over low heat until syrupy. Set aside.
• Return the mille-feuille to the oven to warm through.
• Remove from the oven and, using a knife, carefully release any of the mille-feuille that has become stuck to the baking sheet.
• Lift the mille-feuille off the baking sheet and cut into slices 3 cm x 5 cm x 1 cm.
• Place on a baking sheet then under a moderately hot grill (broiler) to lightly brown the surface.
• Place a small quenelle of the catupiry on a dish and lay a slice of manioc mille-feuille beside it.
• To finish, drizzle some of the Port wine reduction over the mille-feuille and scatter some chopped chives over the dish.

Ants

'Which herbs did you put into this dish?'
'Ants.'
'I would like to know which HERBS you used in the recipe.'
'Son, there's only ants.'

This conversation took place in São Miguel das Cachoeiras in the very north of Brazil. The person asking about the herbs was myself. And the woman answering my questions was Dona Brazi, a member of one of the twenty-three ethnicities that inhabit the region and who sells delicious food in the town's central square. She did not speak Portuguese very well and, after trying her food, I thought she had not understood my question. I wanted to know which herbs and seasonings she had used to make her delicacies. But she had understood perfectly what I was asking. And the answer was simple. The seasoning used in that recipe was ants.

The relationship between man and insect needs to be better understood. Eating insects has always been associated with periods of food shortage, as protein supplementation. Weird, ugly, with no appetite appeal and, generally speaking, not much flavour, insects have always been pushed to the side. In the few instances of urban consumption, they are presented mostly as a tourist attraction.

But the world eats insects without realizing it. For example, they are used to make the cochineal that gives the red tone to the strawberry yogurt you give your kids every day. They also provide red dye to the textile industry. It is our cultural interpretation of the act of taking an insect into our mouths that defines the thin line between the primitive and the modern.

In Brazil, a country nearly as large as the entire USA, there are many records of insect consumption. Not far from the city where I live, São Paulo, is a small region with a particular microclimate. In October, large queen ants more than 3cm long sprout wings and start flying to create new colonies. An old, fun tradition in this region is to run after these ants, catch as many as one can, fry them and eat them

– the last part of their bodies is chubby, like a large ball. They have two names – *içá* is what the local people call them, and *tanajura* is their name given in the caboclo culture, which comprises people of mixed Brazilian native and European ancestry. Brazilian women with generous bottoms are called *tanajuras* too. I don't know if the ants gave the nickname to the women or vice-versa.

The only instance I know of a relationship between man and an edible insect that is not cultural nor a matter of protein supplement occurs in the northernmost tip of the Amazon, on the border between Colombia and Venezuela. The species eaten there are what we call *saúvas* in Brazil and *hormigas limoneiras* in Colombia and Venezuela. It was during one of my trips to the Rio Negro that I met Dona Brazi, with whom I was talking at the beginning of this section. In her city, São Miguel das Cachoeiras, 90 per cent of the population is native. Brazil's official language, Portuguese, is only the second language. The most common language spoken there is Inhangatu, a combination of native languages created by evangelizing priests in an attempt to communicate with the hundreds of tribes in the period of Brazilian colonization.

This region, home to twenty-three ethnic groups speaking twenty-one languages, is one of the most protected areas of the Amazon. The work that anthropologists do here is of crucial relevance for the conservation of the area's natural resources and the possibilities they offer. Just to give an idea, we now know that more than three hundred wild plant species have been domesticated by these ethnic groups. Some have not yet been described by science for use as food. And they risk disappearing, because their use has not been preserved.

One of these ethnic groups, called *tucano*, has a special relationship with the saúva ants. The insect is considered a delicacy and used as a spice would be. Dona Brazi presented me with a reduced tucupi broth. It was purple, almost black, with ants. The first time I tasted it, I was enchanted by the flavours. Dona Brazi's ants have a strong note of lemongrass, supported by ginger and cardamom.

I invited Dona Brazi to come to São Paulo to teach my brigade about the wonders that she produced. She came and stayed with us. It was like receiving a shower of wisdom, a lot of information compressed into a very few words. When I made Dona Brazi try things that do not exist in the Amazon, such as lemongrass and ginger, she laughed and said that they tasted just like ants.

Ants and pineapple

SERVES 4

Ingredients	Preparation	Finish and presentation
Pineapple		
• **1 pineapple**	• Peel the pineapple and cut into 4 equal cubes.	• **4 saúva ants (see page 39)**
		• Place a piece of pineapple on top of a serving dish and top with an ant. Serve immediately.

Langoustine with mini rice and ant powder

SERVES 4

	Ingredients	Preparation	Finish and presentation
Ant powder	• 10 g saúva ants (see page 39) • 10 g dried nori seaweed • 5 g black salt	• Blend the ants, seaweed and black salt in a Thermomix. • Sift and set aside	• Place a generous spoonful of rice in the centre of each of 4 serving plates. • Dust the ant powder over each serving of rice • Place a langoustine beside each serving of rice. • Top the langoustines with the pickled white radish and serve.
Pickled white radish	• 75 ml white wine vinegar • 20 g sugar • 4 g salt • 75 g white radish, peeled and brunoised	• Place the vinegar, sugar and salt in a medium pan over low heat. • When bubbles start to appear around the edge of the pan remove the liquid from the heat, transfer it to a bowl and add the radish. Allow to cool. • Cover the radish and vinegar mixture and transfer to the refrigerator for at least 15 days before using.	
Langoustine broth	• 400 g langoustine heads • 1 leek, finely chopped • 1 celery stick, finely chopped • 1 onion, finely chopped • 1 bay leaf	• Wash the langoustine heads under cold running water. • Place all of the ingredients in a pan over low heat with 1.5 litres of water and heat, without boiling, for 40 minutes. • Strain the broth and set aside.	
Mini rice and langoustine	• 60 g onion, finely chopped • extra virgin olive oil • 250 g mini rice, rinsed • 500 ml langoustine broth (above) • 4 fresh langoustine • salt and pepper	• Preheat the oven to 200°C/400°F. • Fry the onion in a pan with a dash of oil. Stir in the rice and then gradually add the langoustine broth a ladle at a time. Season with salt and pepper. Cook the rice until tender and creamy. Set aside. • Place the langoustines on a tray with a dash of oil. Cook in the preheated oven for 5 minutes. Set aside.	

Cupim and beef

Unlike European and American breeds, 90 per cent of Brazilian cattle are zebu, a native of India whose fat is disposed in an internal layer rather than being marbled throughout. The zebu's main feature is its hump, called cupim in Brazil. This is a reference to the shape of the termite mounds that can be found in uncultivated soil. The cupim cut is very rich in fat and gelatin and is fantastic when prepared with due care and attention. That is not the case in *churrascarias* (meat restaurants), where the meat is cooked at a high temperature and the fat burns very fast.

At D.O.M. we use a two-stage technique to prepare the cupim. The first step is to cook the meat in a steamer in order to melt and expel most of the fat. The result is a rare, almost fat-free meat. I use the broth, rich in flavour and gelatin, as a consommé. As soon as the cupim cools we cook it at a low temperature, to end up with meat so soft and tender that you can eat it with a spoon.

Cupim with potato purée and pequi

	Ingredients	Preparation	Finish and presentation
Cupim	• **2 kg cupim** • **30 g olive oil** • **1 clove garlic** • **1 bay leaf** • **3 onions** • **sea salt**	• Season the cupim with salt and pepper all over. • Heat the oil in a frying pan or skillet, carefully place the meat in the oil and sauté until browned on all sides. • Transfer to a pressure cooker together with the garlic cloves, bay leaf, onions and 1.5 litres of water. Bring to pressure and cook for 2 hours over low heat. • Reduce the pressure naturally at room temperature, then check if the meat is tender. If it is not, bring back to pressure and cook for a while longer until tender. • Remove the meat from the pan and set aside. • Strain the stock, cool and remove the fat. • Check the seasoning, adding some sea salt if necessary, and set aside.	• **the remaining cupim stock** • **the glaze** • **Maldon sea salt** • Preheat the oven to 200°C/400°F. • In a medium pan heat the remaining cupim stock and keep warm. • Cut the meat into slices (about 50 g in weight and 5 cm thick), arrange on a sheet tray, cover with foil and place in the oven for about 5 minutes to warm through. • Remove from the oven and brush with some of the glaze. • Return to the oven for a further 5 minutes. • Remove and brush once more with the glaze. • Place the tray with the meat slices under a grill (broiler) for 30 seconds to finish the glaze. • Place a spoonful of potato-pequi purée on the plate. • Arrange two slices of cupim beside it and scatter some flakes of Maldon salt over each slice. • Drizzle some of the cupim stock around the serving.
Glaze	• **2 onions** • **1 carrot** • **olive oil, for sautéing** • **150 ml madeira wine** • **100 ml cupim stock** • **100 ml beef demi-glace**	• Peel and slice the onions and carrot. • Heat some olive oil in a frying pan or skillet and sauté the vegetables. • Reduce the heat to low, add the Madeira wine and steam for few minutes. • Add the cupim stock and the demi-glace and reduce over low heat for 30 minutes. • Strain and set aside.	
Potato-pequi purée	• **500 g potatoes, clean but unpeeled** • **125 ml double (heavy) cream** • **75 g unsalted butter** • **50 ml pequi oil** • **salt and pepper**	• Fill a large pan with water, add the potatoes, cover and bring to a boil. • Reduce the heat to medium and simmer for 20–25 minutes or until the potatoes are tender. • When the potatoes are cooked, remove from the heat, drain and peel immediately. • Mash the potatoes with a potato masher. • In a large pan heat the heavy (double) cream and butter, then stir in the potatoes. • Add salt and blend with a mixer. • Return to a large pan and mix the pequi oil with the purée. • Check the seasoning and add more salt or pepper if necessary.	

Beef tongue with parsley purée

SERVES 4

	Ingredients	Preparation	Finish and presentation
Beef tongue	• 1 fresh beef tongue, cleaned • 2 sprigs rosemary • 2 sprigs thyme • 2 cloves garlic • 2 bay leaves • 100 g duck fat • salt and pepper	• Season the beef tongue with the rosemary, thyme, garlic, bay leaves, salt and pepper and seal in a vacuum pack. • Cook the sealed tongue for 48 hours at 64°C/147°F in a sous vide. • Remove the tongue from the vacuum pack and use a knife to slice off the skin. • Heat the duck fat in a non-stick pan and fry the tongue for several minutes on both sides. • Slice the tongue into 4 even cubes.	• demi-glace • sea salt • Place a line of parsley purée on a serving plate and top with a cube of the tongue. • Finish with a sprinkling of Maldon salt and a drop of demi glace.
Parsley purée	• 200 g flat leaf parsley • 50 g brazil nuts • 1 clove garlic • 1 cumari pepper • 2 tablespoons red wine vinegar • salt	• Place all of the ingredients in a Thermomix and blend at 60°C/140°F to form a smooth purée. Set aside.	

Sirloin with pickled turnip

SERVES 4

	Ingredients	Preparation	Finish and presentation
Pickled turnip	• **75 ml white wine vinegar** • **20 g sugar** • **4 g salt** • **3 tonka beans** • **4 turnip snowballs, peeled**	• Place the vinegar, sugar, salt and tonka beans in a pan over low heat without boiling. • When bubbles start to form around the edges of the pan remove the liquid from the heat, transfer it to a bowl and add the turnips. • Allow the liquid to cool and then cover and transfer to the refrigerator for at least 15 days before using.	• **1 mangosteen, segmented** • **1 turnip, finely sliced** • **4 chives** • Prepare 4 serving plates. On each plate place 2 pieces of steak and a pickled turnip. • Finish each plate with 2 turnip slices, 2 segments of mangosteen and a chive sprig.
Sirloin	• **480 g wagyu sirloin steak** • **rapeseed (canola) oil** • **salt and pepper**	• Season the steak with salt and pepper. • Heat a cast-iron griddle pan over high heat until smoking and brush it lightly with rapeseed (canola) oil. Pan-fry the steak for several minutes on each side, until cooked on the outside but still pink in the middle. • Place the steak under a preheated grill (broiler) for 2 minutes on each side to finish cooking. • Divide the cooked steak into 8 equal pieces	

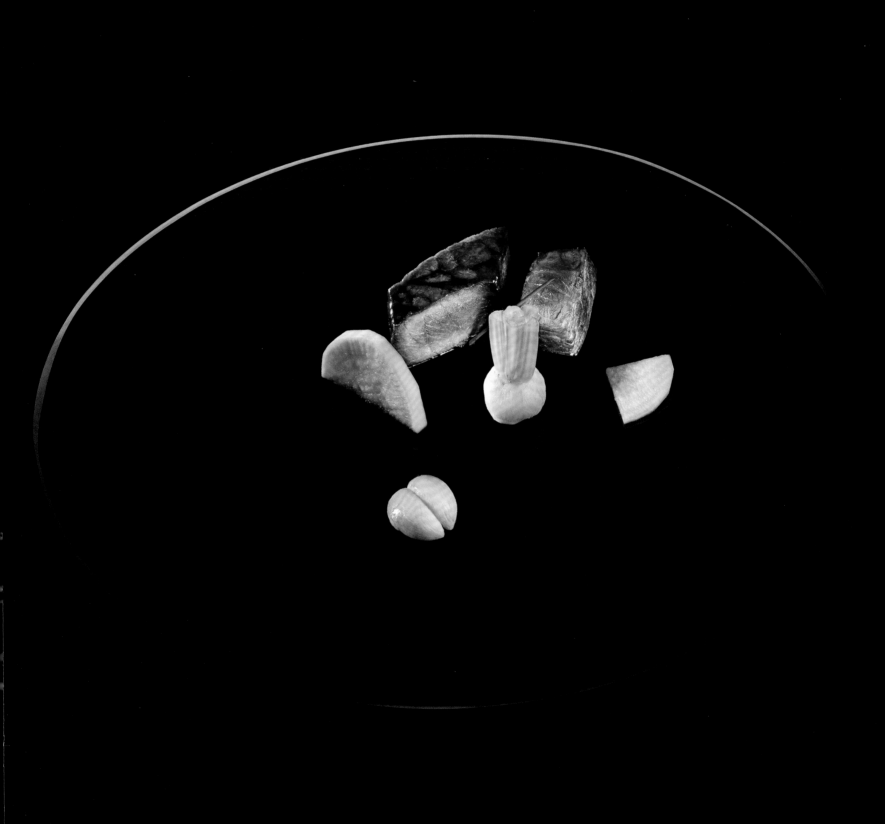

Cured tenderloin with brazil nut milk

	Ingredients	Preparation	Finish and presentation
Cured tenderloin	• **300 g beef tenderloin** • **60 g salt** • **30 g black pepper** • **10 g nutmeg**	• Trim the pieces of tenderloin and make 2 rolls, each 2 cm in diameter and weighing 150 g. • Season with the salt, black pepper and nutmeg, rubbing in well. • Lay each tenderloin on a large piece of clingfilm (plastic wrap), roll up very tightly and tie the ends securely. (This procedure needs to be very well executed in order to achieve a perfect cure.) • Set aside in the refrigerator, set at 6°C/43°F, for a minimum of 8 days before using. Any less will not result in a good cure.	• **black pepper** • **sea salt** • **chives** • **vanilla oil** • Carefully remove the clingfilm from the cured tenderloin. • Cut the meat into slices about 0.5 cm thick and set aside. • Lay the slices of cured meat on one side of the dish and season with black pepper and sea salt. • Add a spoonful of the brazil nut milk in the centre of the dish. • Finish by sprinkling some finely chopped chives over the dish, and add a drizzle of vanilla oil and some slices of the pickled chayote.
Pickled chayote	• **150 g of chayote** • **5 g salt** • **150 g white wine vinegar**	• Using a mandolin, cut the chayote into 1-mm slices. • Combine the salt and vinegar with 50 ml water in a bowl until the salt has dissolved. • Add the sliced chayote, turning it gently with your hands to ensure it is all coated with the pickling mixture. • Cover and set aside in the refrigerator for a week.	
Brazil nut milk	• **100 g brazil nuts, shelled** • **salt**	• Place the brazil nuts in a blender with 300 ml water and liquidize. • Strain through a fine chinois. • Season with a little salt and set aside.	

Cured tenderloin with 100% cocoa from the Amazon

SERVES 4

Ingredients

Cured tenderloin
- 300 g beef tenderloin
- 60 g salt
- 30 g black pepper
- 10 g nutmeg

Chocolate sauce
- 10 g cocoa powder
- 20 g 100% cocoa Amazon chocolate
- 30 ml water
- 25 ml sherry vinegar

Preparation

- Trim the pieces of tenderloin and make 2 rolls, each 2 cm in diameter and weighing 150 g.
- Season with the salt, black pepper and nutmeg, rubbing in well.
- Lay each tenderloin on a large piece of clingfilm (plastic wrap), roll up very tightly and tie the ends securely. (This procedure needs to be very well executed in order to achieve a perfect cure.)
- Set aside in the refrigerator, set at 6°C/43°F, for a minimum of 8 days before using. Any less will not result in a good cure.

- Combine the cocoa powder, the chocolate and the water in a small pan and heat to simmering point.
- Maintain at a simmer until reduced by half.
- Remove from the heat and stir in the sherry vinegar. Set aside.

Finish and presentation

- **black pepper**
- **sea salt**
- **basil oil**

- Carefully remove the clingfilm from the cured tenderloin.
- Cut the meat into 0.5 cm slices and set aside.
- Draw a stripe across the dish with the chocolate sauce.
- Lay the slices of meat on the plate and season with black pepper and some flakes of Maldon salt.
- Finish with a drop of basil oil.

Raw beef with cansanção pesto

Ingredients

Cansanção
pesto

- 5 tablespoons extra virgin olive oil
- 1 clove garlic
- 1 brazil nut
- 1 bunch cansanção, blanched
- salt and pepper

Preparation

- Blend all of the ingredients in a Thermomix until smooth.
- Season with salt and pepper and set aside.

Finish and presentation

- 4 fine slices wagyu beef
- extra virgin olive oil
- black salt and pepper

- Place a slice of beef on the centre of a serving dish.
- Top the beef with a spoonful of cansanção pesto.
- Finish with a sprinkling of black salt and pepper and a drizzle of olive oil.

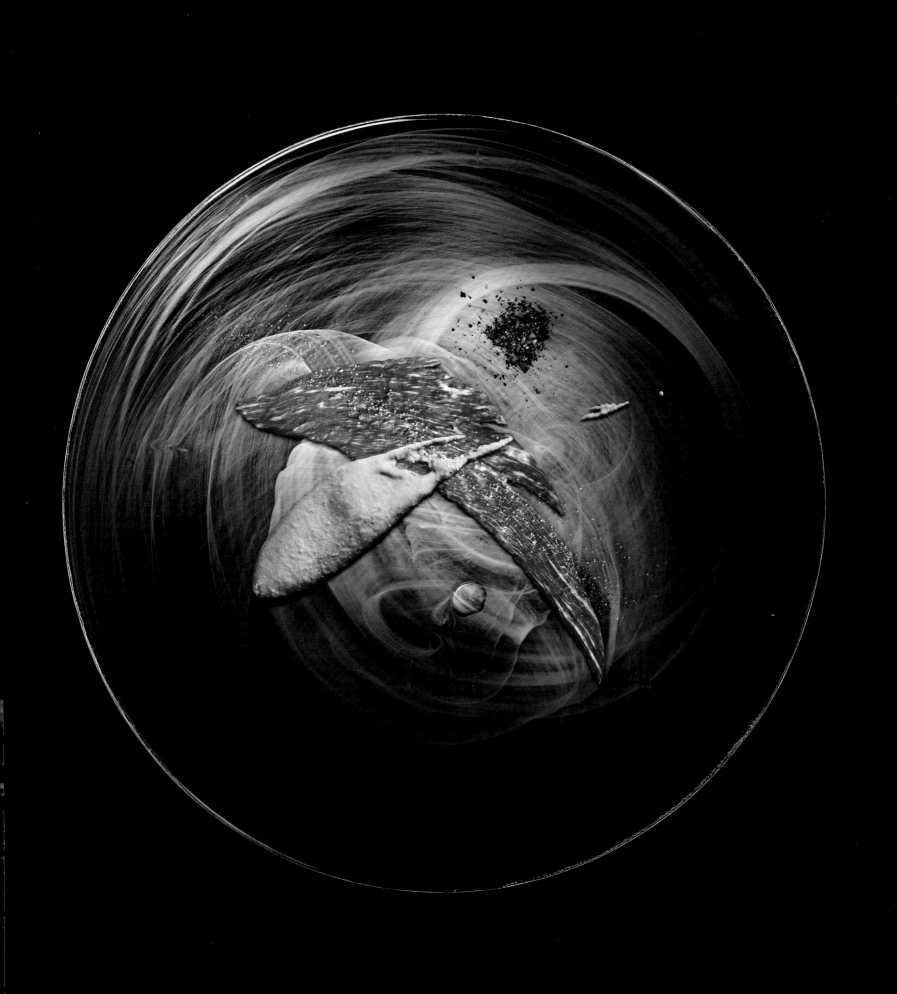

Lamb

Small, resilient and productive; goats are old friends of the Brazilians. But until two decades ago, sheep and goat breeding was limited to the arid zones of the country where the animals were raised in back yards and on small farms.

In the 1990s sheep and goat husbandry gained popularity with the introduction of African and European species and breeding spread to areas of the country with milder climates. With this, the consumption of lamb increased and it started being demanded in markets across Brazil. Initially, only the classical cuts were used: shanks, leg and carré (rack). I have a lot of respect for those cuts but, seeking to find value from the whole animal, we also use secondary cuts such as the kidneys and thymus in the restaurant.

The Brazilian lamb's thymus has great flavour and texture. It is hard to find at market but we have a reliable source and it regularly appears on D.O.M's menu, such as in the recipe for Lamb thymus with artichoke (see page 60).

Lamb thymus with artichoke

	Ingredients	Preparation	Finish and presentation

Artichoke

Ingredients:
- **3 young artichokes**
- **olive oil**
- **1 lime slice**
- **juice of 1 lime**
- **salt and pepper**

Preparation:
- Half and clean 2 of the artichokes.
- Cut them into large pieces, season, and place in a vacuum bag with a dash of olive oil and a slice of lime.
- Cook in a sous vide for 4 hours at 70°C/160°F. Set aside.
- Half and clean the remaining artichoke.
- Using a mandolin, slice very finely .
- Pour the lime juice over the sliced artichoke and set aside.

Finish and presentation:
- **sea salt**
- **olive oil**
- **edible sprouts, to garnish**

- Place the lamb thymus in the centre of a dish.
- Place some slices of artcihoke, both cooked and raw, over the thymus.
- Season with salt and garnish with edible sprouts and chives.

Lamb thymus

Ingredients:
- **200 g lamb thymus**
- **200 ml lamb jus**

Preparation:
- Preheat a grill/broiler.
- Place the lamb thymus under the grill for 2 minutes, turning halfway through.
- Slice the thymus into a small dice and braise over low heat in the lamb jus until tender.

Game meat

Hunting has been banned in Brazil for the past forty years. As we have seen before, well-intentioned environmental legislation can in fact jeopardize the existence of some species that are a part of our culture. After all, man has become part of the natural balance. Conservationist breeding grounds, often with no right to engage in commerce, are the only sources of game meat and for the maintenance of a Brazilian cultural trace. Wildlife management, allied to gastronomic use, may be much more effective to conserving some species than simply prohibiting a part of human culture.

In Brazil we have two kinds of wild pig: *cateto* and *queixada*. *Cateto* is a small, thin pig, with tender meat and a strong gamey flavour. *Queixada* is much bigger: an adult weighs, on average, 40 kilos. Its meat has less personality, but is still very tender.

Maybe the biggest star among Brazilian game is *paca*. A nocturnal, forest-dwelling rodent, it produces a light-coloured meat of inimitable elegance and flavour. It is the most coveted wild delicacy among natives and caboclos, and is mentioned in all the history books that discuss Brazilian food.

We also have two birds in this group of game that deserve a place on the table: duck and pigeon. Even though they are different species from the ones found in Europe, their flavour and texture are virtually identical. But because the Brazilian mallard is not migratory, its meat is more tender than its European counterpart, which makes the flavour more elegant.

Wild boar with plantain purée and aromatic pepper farofa

	Ingredients	**Preparation**	**Finish and presentation**
Herb oil	• 15 g sage • 5 g parsley • 5 g fresh thyme • 2.5 g oregano • 7 g rosemary • 250 ml extra virgin olive oil	• Combine all of the ingredients, cover and leave to infuse in a refrigerator for 1 week.	• 1.5 litres rapeseed (canola) oil • bunch of parsley, chopped • zest of 1 lime • Place the rapeseed (canola) oil in a large pan and heat. • Fry the meat until golden. • Place spoonfuls of the plantain purée and the aromatic pepper farofa on a plate. • Place a portion of wild boar meat on top of the farofa. • Finish with a sprinkling of chopped parsley and some lime zest.
Wild boar	• 600 g wild boar loin • 1 onion, chopped • 2 cloves garlic • 50 ml herb oil (above) • 20 ml white wine • olive oil, for frying • 1 tomato, chopped • 1 onion, chopped • ½ bell pepper chopped • 100 g parsley chopped • 50 g coriander (cilantro) chopped • 1 spicy aromatic pepper • salt	• Cut the meat into 150-g portions. • Place in a bowl and add the chopped onion, garlic, the herb oil, the white wine and some salt and pepper. Mix well. • Cover and place in the refrigerator. Leave for 1 day. • Heat a large pan with a little olive oil. • Remove the meat from the marinade and fry in the pan to seal. • Remove the meat from the pan and set aside on a warmed plate. • Add the tomato, the onion and the bell pepper to the pan and cook over medium heat until softened and amalgamated. • Add the parsley, the coriander (cilantro) and the aromatic pepper. • Return the meat to the pan and top up with water to cover. • Cook until the meat is tender. • Set aside.	
Plantain purée	• 2 plantains • 25 ml extra virgin olive oil • 100 g unsalted butter • salt and pepper	• Peel the plantains and cut into 0.5-cm slices. • Heat the olive oil in a frying pan or skillet and fry the plantain slices. • Transfer the fried plantains to a medium size pan, add a little water and cook for 5 minutes. • Add the butter, transfer to a Thermomix or blender and blend for a few minutes until smooth. • Season with salt and pepper and set aside.	
Aromatic pepper farofa	• 50 g unsalted butter • 100 g manioc flour • 4 aromatic peppers, finely chopped • salt and pepper	• Melt the butter in a large frying pan or skillet. • Add the manioc flour to the pan and incorporate with the melted butter. • Cook, stirring constantly and turning all the contents carefully, until all is toasted and crispy. • Add the chopped aromatic peppers and season with salt and pepper.	

Death

Imagine a masterclass given by a great chef. There he stands in his gleaming whites in front of an audience avid to acquire knowledge. A live chicken enters the scene. The chef, in a tender gesture, picks up the bird and pats its head. Then, in one second, his expression changes. He energetically twists the chicken's neck. It breaks. The animal, still twitching, has its throat cut, and the blood is drained into a bowl. This shocking scene may turn the chef into a savage in the audience's eye, a tyrant.

Curiously, people tend to feel differently where fish are concerned. I have always dreamt of making a video of a newly caught fish being cleaned, cooked and eaten: a cycle with a beginning, middle and end. The idea is to talk about the many faces of the chef that I am: a primitive man, a fisherman, a provider, a transformer, a glutton and a gourmet. This still unmade video sounds lyrical, romantic. But if, instead of fish, I used a chicken or a duck, I would run the risk of being labelled cruel, bloody, ruthless.

When we go to the fishmonger's our eyes travel over fish of many shapes, small and large, over lobsters and other crustaceans – a colourful diversity that attracts us to buy, to cook, to eat. But when we see a photo of a recently killed wild animal, or if we imagine a butcher's shop full of dead calves, cows, goats, lambs, rabbits and pigs, we are repelled.

The only explanation I can propose is that fish change their appearance very little when they die and they keep looking alive. Their shine and freshness make them look clean in our eyes, something that does not happen with other creatures. And the natural lack of expression on a fish may be a contributing factor. Killing chicken, ducks and pigs was part of our recent ancestors' experience – our grandfathers' and grandmothers' experience. And we remember with affection the taste of the food that they made. But modern urban man has distanced himself from basic activities that are necessary before a recipe can be executed. He has lost touch with the termination of a life that many recipes demand.

Jointing and portioning, and neat, hygienic packaging, have cut us off from the rest of reality.

I sometimes amuse myself imagining how it would be if we arrived at our shiny, aseptic supermarkets and found calves, lambs, ducks, still whole, lying exposed on counters. How brutal, violent and dirty such a scene would appear to most of us. I see people buying pieces of chicken breast, fillet mignon, a rack of lamb, without thinking how they would respond if they saw the carcasses of those animals in an abattoir. Similarly, it surprises me that some people feel disgusted by the touch of fresh fish or a raw chicken, but are happy to buy packaged frozen fish fingers or chicken nuggets.

The feeling that is common to all beings, and I include plants here, is the will to keep living. Cut a tree, and it will probably sprout again. Wound an animal, and it will probably crawl away from you, trying to stay alive. As a rational and emotional being, I affirm that nothing justifies taking the life of another being. But we are not only emotional beings. We are, first and foremost, natural beings. As natural beings we are, indeed, omnivores, murderers and selfish. We are human.

The passage from natural man to cultural man goes through the mastery of fire. It is a sign of intelligence to be able to roast a piece of meat.

Death is an element of life, death is an element of cooking, and, even if these words wound you, for each fish, for each piece of meat, perhaps even for each salad you eat, a life has been cut short, directly or indirectly. In the delight we feel, in the pleasure we take in each dish, resides cruelty, something which may also be present in the leather used to make your shoes, in your perfume, in the very paper this book is printed on.

We see each other as human beings, atrocious, greedy, emotional, complacent – we are contradictory. Often pleasure masks cruelty.

The acceptance of these contradictions improves our mutual understanding and our relationships with each other and may even give new meaning to what is life and what is pleasure. Maybe this is a way to return to nature.

The solution I propose is not to judge, and this goes well beyond acceptance. The relationship of human beings with their environment has always been one of extraction, of taking advantage of it. The change I propose is not in our actions, but in our principles. Let us go back. With our human imperfections, we are, and will remain, obliged to extract. We have to re-educate ourselves to go back. To return to nature is a transformative action. And, without a doubt, it is not hedonistic but cultural.

The relationship between man and his food must be rethought. Using the whole of an animal is an important action for tomorrow's world. Respecting nature starts like this. We number more than 7 billion, a species out of control. We have destroyed the balance of our ecosystem. The next deaths may be our own. The relationship between man and his surroundings is advancing towards failure. Our relationship with the primary act of cooking needs to be re-understood if we are to live a sustainable and equitable tomorrow. We need to see ourselves as a natural element, almost like a weed, in relation to our planet. It is in the attitude of the individual, in cultural change, that I see the future of a better cuisine and a better tomorrow.

Fish and shellfish

River fish

When we speak of the Amazon, we are speaking of the largest river basin in the world. And every time we speak of rivers we are also speaking of the sea, since the rivers flow to it. The Amazon basin is one of the most diverse in the planet, thanks to its oceanic proportions. But we — gastronomes, gourmets or gluttons — consider freshwater fish as lesser fish. They are not greatly appreciated. But some Amazon fish deserve a better press. They are:

Filhote is a fish whose name means baby or cub. It is so called because it is the offspring of another fish, the *piraíba*, which can easily reach 200 kilograms. The term *filhote* is used to refer to fish of up to 80 kilograms. From the catfish family, *filhote* has an unmistakable texture, flavour and subtlety.

Pirarucu is the largest of the scaled river fish, and is traditionally preserved in salt. But fresh *pirarucu* is incredible. It is easily adapted to farming, which makes it possible for it to be sold commercially. Farming also creates a better-quality product, with control over size and without the muddy taste of many freshwater fish.

Tucunaré or peacock bass is a hit among big-game fishermen, who come from all over the world to enjoy this type of fishing in the Amazon. Besides attracting tourists, it has great qualities in the kitchen.

Tambaqui is the Amazonian giant, both in size and in flavour. Sustainable fishing of this species can supply another star product to Brazilian cuisine. Unfortunately it has still not adapted well to farming, so its commercial future is still uncertain; but it is easily domesticated. In lakes, its meat develops an earthy flavour. In rivers, the *tambaqui's* natural habitat, it develops a pleasant taste, with a good amount of fat, and allows for a cut that is similar to a fish carré, or, as we call it in Brazil, *costelinha de tambaqui*, or for *tambaqui* ribs (which are used in one of the recipes in this book: see page 90).

Filhote with tucupi

SERVES 4

	Ingredients	Preparation	Finish and Presentation
Bacon flour	• 100 g bacon • **Rapeseed (canola) oil for frying** • 200 g manioc flour (190)	• Cut the bacon in small cubes. • Heat a dash of oil in a frying pan or skillet and fry the bacon on low heat until golden and crisp. Remove from the heat and place on a paper towel to cool. • In a blender, process the bacon until it is turned into powder. • Line a dish with kitchen towel and place the powdered bacon in it. Cover the bacon with kitchen towel and press for 12 hours to remove the fat. • Place the bacon powder and the manioc flour in a bowl, mix well and set aside.	• **flowers, coriander (cilantro), chives and Sechuan buttons, to garnish** • In a medium size pan heat the tucupi-marinated tapioca and place a portion on the bottom of a shallow bowl. • Place a piece of fish beside the tapioca. • Carefully ladle a helping of the hot tucupi broth into the bowl. • Garnish the dish with the sprouts and flowers.
Tucupi broth	• **2.5 litres tucupi (see page 198)** • **50 ml fish fumet** • **50 g chopped onion** • **30 g coriander (cilantro)** • **8 Amazonian peppers, chopped** • **salt**	• In a pan place the tucupi, fumet, onion, coriander (cilantro) and Amazonian pepper with 50 ml water. • Simmer on low heat for about 20 minutes. Do not let it boil. • Season with salt and set aside.	
Tapioca	• **200 g tapioca** • **100 ml tucupi broth (above)**	• Bring a large pan of water to the boil. Carefully pour in the tapioca and cook for about 45 minutes, or until it is nearly transparent (you will see a small white dot inside). • Strain and place in a bowl with 100 ml of the the tucupi broth to marinate for at least 30 minutes.	
Filhote fish	• **4 fillets of filhote fish, about 150 g each** • **20 g bacon flour (above)** • **Rapeseed (canola) oil** • **salt and pepper**	• Preheat the oven to 200°C/400°F. • Season the fish with salt and pepper. Coat one side of the fish with the bacon flour. • Place a dash of oil in a non-stick frying pan or skillet and fry the floured side of the fish first until deep golden and crispy. Turn and quickly seal the other side of the fish. • Place on a baking sheet and put in the preheated oven for 2 minutes.	

Tambaqui ribs with tripe and sausage

SERVES 4

	Ingredients	Preparation	Finish and presentation
Herb oil	• **15 g sage** • **5 g parsley** • **5 g fresh thyme** • **2.5 g oregano** • **7 g rosemary** • **250 ml olive oil**	• Place all the ingredients in a vacuum pack. • Place the pack in the sous-vide at 8°C and infuse for 30 days.	• **sea salt** • Ladle a spoonful of the tomato sauce with tripe, sausage and beans into a deep bowl. • Place a portion of tambaqui ribs in the centre of the bowl. • Sprinkle over some sea salt and serve.
Tripe	• **250 ml extra virgin olive oil** • **250 g tripe** • **1 bay leaf** • **salt and pepper**	• Clean the tripe under running water. • Season the tripe and place in a large pan with a bay leaf. • Add enough water to just cover the tripe and bring to a boil over medium heat. • Cook for around 1 hour, or until tender. • Remove the tripe from the pan, slice finely and set aside.	
Broad beans	• **300 g broad (fava) beans**	• Cook the broad (fava) beans over low heat with plenty of water for about 30 minutes or until tender. Strain and reserve.	
Tomato sauce	• **1 small onion, finely chopped** • **2 cloves garlic, chopped** • **olive oil** • **2 paio sausages, chopped** • **prepared tripe (above)** • **200 ml white wine** • **2 tablespoons herb oil (above)** • **200 ml passata (puréed canned tomatoes)** • **broad beans (above)**	• In a large pan, braise the onion and the garlic with a little bit of oil. • Add the chopped sausage and sliced tripe to the pan and pan fry for 3 minutes. • Add the white wine and leave to cook for a few minutes more. • Add the herb oil and passata, stir to combine, and cook for 10 minutes more. • Set aside and keep warm, stirring through the broad beans just before serving.	
Tambaqui ribs	• **420 g tambaqui ribs** • **olive oil**	• Preheat the oven to 200°C/400°F. • Season the tambaqui ribs with salt and pepper. • Heat a drop of oil in a frying pan or skillet and pan-fry the ribs on one side until light brown. • Place the ribs on a baking sheet and transfer to the oven for 3 minutes to finish cooking.	

Sea fish

Brazil has one of the longest coasts of the planet. We have more than 4,000 miles (7,000 kilometres) of Atlantic beaches, from Cape Orange in the north to Chuí on the border with Uruguay in the extreme south. The measurement would go up to 5,500 miles (9,000 kilometres) if you took into account the Brazilian coast's recesses and protuberances, which include beaches, mangroves, dunes, reefs, bays and spits.

This extensive and abundant coast is full of diversity. In the south, very near Argentina, the waters are colder and there are a great variety of fish and bivalves to be found. As you travel farther north, the diversity of bivalves and crustaceans decreases and tropical fish prevail. I would not compare our fish to the cold water fish so abundant in the northern hemisphere, but I do grant them special attention and they feature heavily in the food that we cook at D.O.M..

Cod with bone marrow

SERVES 4

	Ingredients	**Preparation**
Bone marrow	• 500 g bone marrow bones, cut into 5 cm lengths	• Soak the bones in salted ice water for 2 hours, changing the water every 30 minutes. • Scoop the marrow from the bone and place in salted ice water for another 2 hours, changing the water every 30 minutes. • Slice the marrow into fine strips, cover and place in the refrigerator until needed.
Crispy cod skin	• skin from 1 medium cod • 1 tablespoon rapeseed (canola) oil	• Dehydrate the skin in the oven or dehydrator for 6 hours at 60°C/140°F. • Heat the oil in frying pan or skillet until it reaches 150°C/300°F. • Fry the cod skin until crispy in the oil, making sure that the skin does not colour. • Remove from the pan and set aside.
Salt cod	• 1 salt cod loin, skin on • extra virgin olive oil	• Wash the cod under running water to remove the excess of salt. • Place the cod in a bowl of water and transfer to the refrigerator to desalt for 3 days, changing the water every 8 hours. • Slice the cod in 100 g portions. • Put the cod inside a vacuum bag with a splash of extra virgin olive oil. • Cook in a sous vide at 60°C/40°F for 8 minutes. • Remove from the bag and set aside with the juice from the bag.
Kale	• 250 g kale • 2 cloves garlic, finely minced • 1 tablespoon bacon fat • rapeseed (canola) oil, for deep frying • salt	• Finely chop 200 g of the kale. Blanch in boiling water for a few seconds and drain. • Heat the bacon fat in a frying pan or skillet and briefly fry the garlic. • Add the chopped kale to the pan and cook for a few seconds. Season with salt and set aside, keeping warm. • Heat the (rapeseed) canola oil in a fat fryer to 180°C/350°F. • Tear the remaining 50 g of kale and place in the fat fryer for around 2 minutes, until crispy. Set aside.

Finish and presentation

• extra virgin olive oil
• 4 tablespoons beef demi-glace
• salt and pepper

• In a small pan, warm the juice that the salt cod was cooked in.
• Transfer the broth to a bowl and, whilst beating with an electric hand mixer, gradually add olive oil to form a thin mayonnaise.
• Warm the demi-glace in a small pan.
• Heat a drop of olive oil in a frying pan or skillet and pan fry the salt cod on the skin side until crispy.
• Place the bone marrow under a preheated grill (broiler) to warm.
• Place a tablespoon of demi-glace on the centre of a plate and top with a piece of cod.
• Place a spoonful of the sautéed kale on the plate beside the fish and a piece of the bone marrow beside it.
• Dress the dish with a few drops of the cod mayonnaise and ganish with pieces of dried cod skin and deep-fried kale.

Sardine with oyster mayonnaise

SERVES 4

	Ingredients	Preparation	Finish and Presentation
Oyster mayonnaise	• 5 oysters, shucked • 20 g black olive oil • rapeseed (canola) oil • salt and pepper	• Place the oysters in a large bowl with the black olive oil. Using a hand mixer blend till smooth and well combined. • Gently stir in a little rapeseed (canola) oil, a few drops at a time, until the mixture resembles mayonnaise. • Season with salt and pepper, cover and set aside in the refrigerator.	• 2 tomatoes • chives, finely chopped • 100 g lardons, finely sliced and fried until crisp
Sardines	• 4 fresh sardine fillets • salt and pepper	• Season the sardine fillets with salt and pepper. • Heat a non-stick frying pan or skillet and cook the fillets for 3 minutes on the skin side only. Set aside.	• Cut the tomatoes in half, discard the seeds and remove the pulp. Set the pulp aside. • Place a spoonful of chives on the centre of a plate. • Lay a sardine fillet skin side down on the chopped chives. • Place a spoonful of the oyster mayonnaise on the dish beside the sardine fillet and decorate with the tomato pulp.

Rice with grouper

SERVES 4

	Ingredients	Preparation	Finish and Presentation
Fish broth	• 1 x 2-kg grouper • 200 g onions, halved	• Scale the fish, reserving the scales. • Fillet the fish and separate the head and the carcass. • Place the fish head, carcass and the halved onions in a pan with 3 litres of water. • Bring to the boil and continue to boil for 5 minutes. • Reduce the heat and simmer until the broth is reduced to 1.5 litres. Drain through a sieve (strainer) and set aside.	• **juice of 1 lime** • **olive oil** • **chervil** • **salt and pepper** • Place a serving of rice in the centre of the plate and arrange the fish cubes over it. • Finish with some lime juice and a drizzle of olive oil, then scatter some fried fish scales and chervil over the dish.
Fish scales	• fish scales from the grouper • 2 tablespoons olive oil	• Wash the fish scales thoroughly and let them dry. • In a frying pan or skillet heat the oil then fry the scales until they are golden and crispy. Set aside.	
Rice	• olive oil • 60 g onion, chopped • 250 g rice	• Add a dash of oil to a clean frying pan or skillet and fry the chopped onion. • Add the rice, and then slowly add the fish broth. Season with salt and cook until the rice is tender.	
Grouper	• grouper fillets (above) • olive oil • salt and pepper	• Cut the fish into small cubes and season with salt and pepper. • Add a little oil to a frying pan or skillet and fry the fish until golden.	

Needlefish ceviche

SERVES 4

	Ingredients	Preparation	Finish and Presentation
Radish powder	• **250 g red radish**	• Cut the radish into small dice and place in the Pacojet cup. Cover and place in the freezer for 24 hours. • Grind briefly in the Pacojet machine.	• **radish powder** • **celery sprouts** • **jiquitaia pepper**
Tiger's milk	• **200 ml lime juice** • **120 g grouper fish** • **½ fresh hot chilli pepper** • **20 g chilli powder** • **30 g celery** • **30 g onion**	• Mix the chilli powder with the lime juice in a bowl. • Finely chop the fish, fresh chilli pepper, celery and onion then add them to the lime juice mixture and marinate for 8 minutes. • Place in the Pacojet and grind, then strain the juice through a fine sieve into a bowl and reserve.	• Place a serving of the needle fish ceviche on a plate and arrange some slices of heart of palm over it. • Finish with a sprinkling of radish powder, some celery sprouts and a pinch of jiquitaia pepper.
Needlefish ceviche	• **200 g heart of palm** • **5 fillets needle fish, cut in 2 cm strips** • **30 g red onion, sliced** • **tiger's milk (see above)** • **salt**	• Using a mandoline, cut the heart of palm in very thin slices. • In a bowl mix the fish and the onion together and season with the tiger's milk and salt.	

Squid rice

SERVES 4

	Ingredients	Preparation	Finish and presentation

Herb oil

- **15 g sage**
- **5 g parsley**
- **5 g fresh thyme**
- **2.5 g oregano**
- **7 g rosemary**
- **250 ml extra virgin olive oil**

• Combine all of the ingredients, cover and leave to infuse in a refrigerator for 1 week.

Finish and presentation

- **edible sprouts, to decorate**

• Divide the rice between 4 serving bowls and garnish each with an edible sprout. Serve immediately.

Squid rice

- **350 g fresh squid**
- **250 g rice**
- **3 cloves garlic, finely chopped**
- **50 ml white wine**
- **extra virgin olive oil**
- **salt and pepper**

• Clean the squid and separate the bodies from the tentacles. Remove the head and beak and discard, retain the ink sack and tentacles.
• Add the rice to the pan and allow to cook for a few minutes. Add the white wine and cook until reduced. Add 500 ml cold water to the pan, stir once, and leave to cook.
• When the rice is almost cooked, add the squid and mix well. Cook for 3 minutes and then remove from the heat. Season with salt, pepper and a drizzle of extra virgin olive oil.

Bivalves

In Brazil we have a flat-shelled mangrove oyster, *Crassostrea brasiliensis* or *brasiliana*, which, because of the unique ecosystem it grows in, carries an elegant mangrove note. It reaches an impressive size and is very meaty. It is still rare to find it in Brazilian supermarkets because a non-native variety from Japan, *Crassostrea gigas*, is more popular. This oyster has a meaty texture and a slightly milky taste. Its cultivation in Brazil, besides being a great contribution to gastronomy, also helps to boost the income of coastal populations. The same occurs in the case of mussels, which are abundant in the south of the country.

In the north of Brazil, the size of bivalve molluscs decreases significantly, with many growing to be no larger than a fingernail. I especially like those called *sururu*, a tiny mussel, and *maçunim*, a species of cockle, both of which are endemic of salt-water lagoons and are primarily used to make tasty broths.

Another Brazilian mollusc is the *lambreta*, a relative of the clam that is found in the mangrove swamps of the north-eastern region of Bahia. It is fatty, meaty and very tasty and deserves to become a more valued ingredient in the Brazilian larder.

Scallops with coconut milk, aromatic pepper and crispy mango

SERVES 4

	Ingredients	Preparation	Finish and presentation
Aromatic pepper oil	• **200 g aromatic pepper** • **30 ml cachaça** • **15 ml white vinegar** • **1 bunch rosemary** • **1 bay leaf** • **1 clove garlic** • **750 ml canola oil**	• Place all the ingredients in a vacuum pack. • Place the pack in the sous-vide at 8°C and infuse for 30 days.	• Arrange 3 scallops in a soup plate and pour a little of the coconut milk marinade over them. • Garnish with one mango crispy, some coriander sprouts and the fresh aromatic pepper.
Mango crispies	• **1 vanilla pod** • **150 g fresh mango, stone and skin removed** • **44 g glucose**	• Preheat the oven to 130°C. • Cut the vanilla pod lengthwise and scrape out the seeds. • Place the mango and the vanilla seeds in a blender and process. • Pass through a fine sieve into a clean bowl and set aside. • In a small pan over low heat melt the glucose and stir it into the mango and vanilla mixture. • Spread the mixture in very thin layers on a silpat and bake for 35-40 minutes, or until crunchy. Store in a cool, dry place.	
Scallops	• **12 scallops (cleaned)** • **25 ml lemon juice** • **150 ml coconut milk** • **10 ml aromatic pepper oil** • **10 g mint leaves** • **salt**	• Place the scallops in a bowl and place in a bain-marie filled with ice. • Add the lemon juice and some salt, mix together and marinate for 2 minutes. • Add the coconut milk and the aromatic pepper oil. Mix thoroughly. • Cut the mint leaves into chiffonade and add to the mixture.	

Blue mussels with cariru

SERVES 4

	Ingredients	**Preparation**	**Finish and presentation**

Blue mussels

- **30 g extra virgin olive oil**
- **1 clove garlic, chopped**
- **300 g blue mussels**
- **50 ml white wine**
- **50 ml water**

• Heat the olive oil in a large pan and sauté the garlic until light golden brown.
• Add the blue mussels, the white wine and the water. Cover and cook until the mussels open.
• Strain the liquid into a clean bowl.
• Remove the mussels from their shells and reserve the shells.
• Place the mussels in the bowl with the reserved liquid in which they were cooked and set aside in the refrigerator.

Cariru cream

- **220 g cariru**
- **55 g onion confit**
- **110 g vegetable stock**
- **salt**

• Half fill a bowl with ice and cover the ice with cold water. Place another bowl in this ice bath to chill.
• Bring a large pan of salted water to a boil and blanch the cariru for 30 seconds.
• Transfer immediately to the ice bath to stop the cooking process. Strain well.
• Transfer the cariru to the Thermomix, add the onion confit and the vegetable stock and blend until it forms a homogeneous purée.
• Strain again but do not press the purée. Set aside the strained juice and the purée in separate containers.

Finish and presentation

- **white edible flowers**
- **cariru sprouts**
- **black salt and pepper**

• Place the mussels with their stock in a large pan and heat through.
• Season with salt and pepper.
• Place some cariru cream on a plate.
• Place a mussel in its shell on the plate beside the cream, adding a small amount of cariru juice around the shellfish.
• Finish with a few grains of black salt, and decorate with white flowers and cariru sprouts.

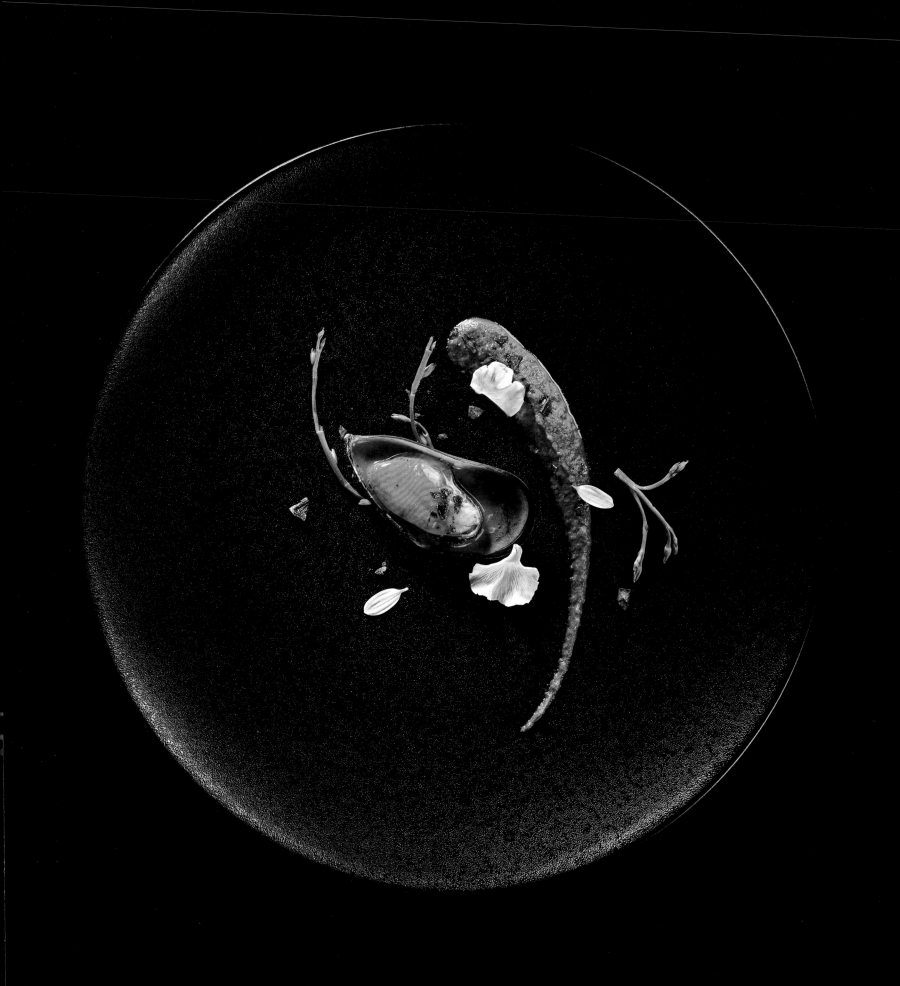

Sea Snail

The warm waters off the Brazilian coast are home to fish with thinner fat layers than the ones found in the colder waters around Europe, much of North America and Chile. From a gastronomic point of view our seafood and fish require a different understanding. This is why I take great care when shopping for them.

My sous-chef, Geovane Carneiro, and I are responsible for our daily fish purchases. We have developed a close relationship with our fish supplier, Marcelo Nomaka. It was Marcelo who introduced us to the Brazilian sea snail, a byproduct of shrimp fishing that can be found all year round along the coastline.

I am a fan of snails and clams — escargots, vongole and all their variations — and I had always resented the fact that I lived in an area with poor choices in this department. But now it would be a different story. I proceeded to cook the Brazilian sea snails as taught by the classic culinary texts: I marinated it, pre-cooked it, then sliced and grilled it. This was the best saltwater snail I had ever tasted. It is a shame that Brazilian shrimp fishermen catch it in their nets but throw it away, which makes it difficult for chefs to find on a regular basis.

Sea snail with wakame and tangerine foam

	Ingredients	**Preparation**	**Finish and presentation**
Sea snail	• **400 g sea snail** • **50 ml of white vinegar** • **1 bay leaf** • **4 spoons coarse salt** • **3 cloves garlic** • **160 g diced onions**	• Place the sea snails in a bowl and cover with water, then add the vinegar and the salt. Place in the refrigerator for 12 hours. • At the end of this time, strain the snails from the soaking liquid and place in a large pan. • Cover with water, then add the bay leaf, salt, garlic and onions. Cook for approximately 4 hours or until the snails are tender. • Drain the snails and place in a covered container in the refrigerator.	• **olive oil** • **150 g wakame, rehydrated in water** • **garlic, chopped** • **1 tangerine supreme** • **edible flowers for decoration** • **tangerine rind** • **salt and pepper**
Sauce	• **200 g fish bones** • **100 ml demi-glace**	• Preheat the oven to 180°C/350°F. • Place the fish bones in a roasting pan and roast for 10 minutes. • Place the demi-glace and the fish bones in a medium-sized pan and cook for 30 minutes over medium heat (do not boil), then strain through a fine sieve and reserve.	• Cut each sea snail in three parts and season with salt and pepper. • Heat some olive oil in a frying pan or skillet and seal the snails over medium heat. Remove and set aside on a warm dish.
Tangerine foam	• **50 ml concentrated tangerine juice** • **10 g of soy lecithin**	• In an electric blender, combine the ingredients with 250 ml of water to make a foam.	• In the same frying pan or skillet, sauté the wakame with some chopped garlic. • Place a spoonful of sauce in a soup plate, then pile up a serving of sea snails on the sauce and arrange some of the wakame beside it. • Place a spoonful of the tangerine foam over the dish and decorate with pieces of the tangerine supreme, the flowers and a tangerine twist.

A treatise on caipirinha

Caipirinha is one of the drinks that are most representative of Brazil. It became famous some time ago, and variations on it have been created both at home and around the world.

Instead of using cachaça, people started substituting vodka and saké. I have nothing against variations on themes, but they should not be given the same name as the original. The true caipirinha is made with cachaça, lime, ice and cane sugar. At D.O.M.'s bar, we have developed an impeccable ritual which I shall share with you here. We also prepare caipirinha derivatives. And I especially like the one that uses limão-cravo, limão-rosa, passion fruit, mint, priprioca (see page 186) and, of course, the essential cachaça.

Lime

The ideal lime for caipirinha is thin-skinned and soft. Lemon skins are too thick for caipirinha, even though their capacity for oxidation and their incredible aroma are great to add a final twist.

The skin of the lime is important for flavouring the drink. At D.O.M. we cut the tips off the lime, then cut it in half and delicately slit the outer part of the skin. D.O.M.'s caipirinha looks like a lime sashimi. It is not true that the inside of the lime makes the drink bitter; but neither does it contribute to the drink's looks. A good drink must look good as well as taste good. Avoid crushing the lime too much. Three or four turns with the reamer are enough, after you make the slits on the skin.

Sugar

One of the characteristics of cane sugar is that it is made of crystals, which rarely dissolve completely in the cachaça. We solved this problem by making a sugar syrup. We use 700 grams of regular refined sugar, or caster sugar, per half a litre of water. We boil the water, then turn off the heat. We add the sugar, stir vigorously and produce a temperature shock by adding ice cubes. We use about 50 ml of this syrup in each caipirinha.

Glass   At D.O.M., we use Old Fashioned glasses to serve caipirinha.

Ice   We use seven ice cubes per glass. They must be crystal-clear, which means they must have the lowest possible oxygen content.

Cachaça   We have a huge range of cachaças in Brazil. Good caipirinha is made with good cachaça. The caboclos from Minas Gerais – the state which produces Anísio Santiago, the most esteemed cachaça in the country, which is left to age for twelve years – say that good cachaça is one that produces 'pearl necklaces'. How so? Shake the cachaça bottle. It must form a ring of bubbles where the drink ends, below the cork. If it is a good cachaça, the bubbles will be small. Big bubbles are a sign of inferior quality. There are some cachaça counterfeiters who use lye to cause the same effect.

So take note of some of the places where good cachaça is made. Minas Gerais produces good cachaça, especially in the towns of Salinas, Januária, Ponte Nova e a Paracatu. In Rio de Janeiro, the ones from Paraty are the best. Pernambuco, Ceará and São Paulo also produce good liquor. Oh, and caipirinhas made with good cachaça do not cause hangovers!

Vegetables
and roots

Pumpkin

Although pumpkins grow all over the world, in Brazil we have a variety that I consider very special. We call it *abóbora-de-pescoço*, or neck-pumpkin. The name comes from its shape, reminiscent of a figure 8 with an elongated waist or long neck. It has an incomparable texture and flavour and can even be eaten raw, so delicate and sweet that it is. And this variety offers a bonus: sprouts called *cambuquira*, they are widely used in Brazilian kitchens. In my view, they are tastier than the flowers, which, as with European varieties, can also be used in recipes.

Pumpkin, vegetable coal and tapioca ice cream

SERVES 4

	Ingredients	Preparation	Finish and Presentation
			• **edible flowers** • **smoked salt**
Tapioca ice cream	• 250 ml whole milk • 25 g granulated tapioca • 200 ml double (heavy) cream • 12.5 g caster (superfine) sugar • 15 g ice cream stabilizer • 50 ml coconut milk • 100 g sweetened condensed milk	• Place 200 ml of the milk in a bowl, mix the tapioca into it and leave to soak for 30 minutes. • Transfer the mixture to a large pan and add the cream, sugar, stabilizer, coconut milk and sweetened condensed milk. Cook over low heat until the temperature reaches 80°C/175°F. • Leave to soak for 9 hours. • After this period, add the remaining 50 ml of milk to the cream mixture, transfer to an ice cream maker and blend.	• Drain the sweet squash pieces thoroughly. • With the aid of a blowtorch, char one side of the squash pieces and then brush lightly with pepper syrup. • Sprinkle charred herbs onto the bottom of a serving dish. • Place some pieces of squash on the charred herbs and beside it place a helping of rock sugar and a scoop of coconut foam. • Sprinkle smoked salt over the foam. • Finish with a quenelle of tapioca ice cream and garnish with flowers.
Sweet squash	• 250 g abóbora pescoço squash (see page 134) • 100 g quicklime (see page 284) • 500 g sugar • 1 aromatic red pepper • 1 cinnamon stick • rind of 2 oranges	• Peel and cut the squash into 2.5-cm cubes. • Dissolve the quicklime carefully in 1 litre of water. Place the squash in the mixture and leave to soak for three hours. • Remove the squash from the quicklime solution and wash thoroughly in running water. • In a large pan, place 1 litre of water, the sugar, pepper, cinnamon and orange rinds. • Place over low heat (do not boil) until it reaches 100°C/200°F. • Add the washed squash and simmer over low heat for two hours. • Cool, cover and set aside in the refrigerator.	
Charred herbs	• 5 g rosemary • 5 g salvia • 5 g coriander (cilantro) • 5 g sweet chervil • 5 g basil • 5 g parsley	• Preheat the oven to 200°C/400°F. • Wrap all the herbs in a sheet of aluminum foil and bake for one hour, then increase the heat to 250°C/480°F and bake for 30 minutes more. • Place the charred herbs in the bowl of the Thermomix and process into a powder. • Pass the powder through a fine sieve and set aside.	
Charred herb and coconut foam	• 10 g sugar • 62 ml coconut milk • 2 g leaf gelatine • 2.5 g charred herbs (above) • 5 g egg white powder	• Combine the sugar and coconut milk with 30 ml of water in a small pan. • Over low heat, allow the mixture to reach 100°C/200°F, then cool to 70°C /160°F. • Meanwhile place the gelatine in a little cold water to rehydrate. Add it with the charred herbs and the egg white powder to the coconut milk mixture and beat with a mixer until all the ingredients are combined. • Pass through a sieve (strainer), place in a siphon and whip with 2 gas charges. • Set aside to rest in the refrigerator for 2 hours.	
Pepper syrup	• 100 g sugar • 2 red Brazilian peppers	• In a small pan add the sugar and peppers to 100 ml of water and simmer over 120°C/250°F heat to make a syrup.	
Rock sugar	• 21 g icing (confectioners') sugar • 5 g egg white powder • 1 g edible gold dust • 1.5 g bicarbonate of soda (baking soda) • 64 g sugar • 36 ml water	• Place the icing (confectioners') sugar, egg white powder, gold dust and bicarbonate of soda (baking soda) in a bowl and set aside. • In a pan dissolve the sugar in the water and make a 136°C/275°F simple syrup. • Add the icing (confectioners') sugar mixture gently to the syrup and combine thoroughly. The mixture will double in volume. • Spread it onto a Silpat sheet and leave to cool. • Break the rock into small pieces approximately 2 cm across then place in a food dehydrator at 70°C/160°F for one hour.	

Yam

Yams and carás are readily found in Brazilian grocery stores and are commonly used in baby food, because it is believed that they are important for growth. From this giant tuberous root I produce a velvety, silky purée. It can be insipid, but precisely for that reason, it makes a great base for other potent and more dominant flavours. Sometimes I use it to calm rich flavours such as fish eggs, strong reductions, and offal such as kidney and liver. At other times I take advantage of its neutrality and use it as a base for delicate-flavoured herbs and vegetables, or even for a simple flavoured salt, such as cod salt. I like the effect of white on white: the limited visual information does not reflect the elegance of the delicate flavours that the customer is about to taste.

Lamb kidney with pineapple, yam purée and priprioca

SERVES 4

	Ingredients	Preparation	Finish and presentation
Yam purée	• **1 kg yams** • **300 ml whole milk** • **80 g unsalted butter** • **200 ml double (heavy) cream** • **salt and pepper**	• Bring a large pan of salted water to the boil, enough to cover the yams completely, and cook them whole in their skins until soft. • Drain and peel the yams and chop finely. • Place in a Thermomix with the milk and beat well. • Place the butter and cream in a large pan and melt over low heat. Stir in the yam mixture and cook for 20 minutes more, stirring occasionally. Season to taste.	• **4 edible sprouts** • Spoon a portion of the lamb kidney into a bowl. • Place a spoonful of yam purée beside it. • Garnish with an edible sprout and serve.
Lamb kidney with pineapple	• **3 very fresh lamb kidneys** • **rapeseed (canola) oil** • **200 g pearl onions, peeled and quartered** • **150 g pineapple, cubed** • **300 ml Lamb jus** • **Priprioca essence, to taste** • **salt and pepper**	• Trim the kidneys to remove any membranes or blood vessels that look unappetizing. Season with salt and pepper. • Heat a drop of rapeseed (canola) oil in a frying pan or skillet and pan-fry the kidneys over high heat until light brown. Turn and fry the other side. • Add the onions and lamb jus to the pan and cook for 3 minutes more. • Remove from the heat, add the pineapple and priprioca essence to taste. • Season the dish and set aside.	

Baroa potato

Another important tuberous root – regarded as the most important by foreign chefs living in Brazil – is *mandioquinha*, or *batata-baroa*. Close to the potato family, and largely used in everyday home cooking where it is one of the main bases for baby food, it has a velvety texture, a powerful, slightly sweet flavour and a distinctive yellow colour

Ray fish with Brazilian butter, lemon thyme and smoked baroa potato

SERVES 4

	Ingredients	Preparation	Finish and Presentation
Peanut foam	• **100 g peanuts** • **2 g lecithin**	• In an electric blender process the nuts and lecithin with 300 ml water until well combined.	• **smoked salt** • **10 ml demi-glace**
Baroa potato	• **1 kg coarse salt** • **200 g baroa potato**	• Preheat the oven to 200°C/400°F. • Dampen the coarse salt and scatter half of it on the bottom of a roasting pan, then place the baroa potato on top. Scatter the rest of the coarse salt over the potato and bake for one hour. • Cool, then remove the salt, peel the skin off the potatoes and cut each of them into 4 long pieces.	• Using an electric mixer, beat the peanut mixture to make a foam. • Place a dash of warm demi-glace in the centre of a plate. • Place the ray fish on top of the demi-glace. • Arrange the broccoli and the baroa potato beside the ray fish. • Garnish with a scoop of the peanut foam and sprinkle some smoked salt over the baroa potato.
Lemon thyme butter	• **50 g butter** • **2 sprigs lemon thyme**	• Place the butter and the lemon thyme in a small pan. • Melt the butter briefly over low heat, leave to infuse for 5 minutes then sieve through a chinois and set aside.	
Ray fish and broccoli	• **60 g broccoli** • **30 g Brazilian butter (see page 26)** • **600 g ray fish** • **lemon thyme butter (above)** • **2 sprigs lemon thyme** • **baroa potato (above)** • **salt and pepper**	• Cut the broccoli into little branches. Bring a medium-sized pan of water to the boil and cook the broccoli briefly. Set aside. • Melt the Brazilian butter in a non-stick frying pan or skillet over gentle heat. • Carefully place the ray fish in the pan and cook for a few minutes, then turn over. • Remove from the heat and place the lemon thyme butter on top of the fish and sprinkle a few leaves of fresh lemon thyme over it. • In the same pan, using the juices from the fish, sautée the broccoli and the baroa potato for a few seconds.	

Mangarito

Another tuberous root that we use is mangarito, which is in danger of becoming extinct. Despite its unique texture and wild flavour, it became regarded as a a dull ingredient in home cooking. It was gradually substituted for similar ingredients in everyday recipes. Due to this lack of popularity, it almost disappeared from the shelves of supermarkets and plantations. There have been many initiatives to revive this tuberous root, but none has had any effect yet.

Prawns with mangarito and purple yam

SERVES 4

	Ingredients	Preparation	Finish and presentation
Mangorito and yam	• 250 g mangarito • 250 g purple yam • 2 kg coarse salt	• Preheat the oven to 200°C/400°F. • Spread 500 g of the salt over the base of a roasting pan and dampen with water. • Place the mangarito on the salt, cover with another 500 g of salt and dampen the top layer with water. • Repeat this process in a separate roasting pan with the purple yam and remaining salt. • Bake the mangarito and yam in the oven for 1 hour and set aside to cool. • Remove the salt from the mangarito and slice each one into 4. Set aside. • Remove the salt from the yams, peel off the salt and slice them finely into rounds. Set aside.	• 1 orange, zested and segmented • beldroega sprigs • sea salt • Place a portion of the prawns in the centre of a plate. • Place the mangarito and purple yam on the plate next to the prawns. • Garnish with an orange segment and orange zest, sprigs of beldroega and sea salt.
Prawns (shrimp)	• 500 g fresh prawns (shrimp) • 3 tablespoons extra virgin olive oil • zest of 1 lime	• Clean and shell the prawns (shrimp), reserving the heads. • Season the shrimp with salt and pepper. • Heat a frying pan or skillet and pan fry the prawn heads with the olive oil for 5 minutes. • Remove the heads from the pan and discard. Using the same pan and oil, pan fry the prawns until pink. • Add the lime zest and remove from the heat. Remove the prawns from the pan, set aside and reserve the sauce.	

Okra

The most important movement for global gastronomy was, without a doubt, the great navigations of the Age of Discoveries. Of African origin, okra was brought to Brazil and we took it as our own. During one of my journeys around the world I once prepared a recipe which is almost a signature dish, called *okra, okra, okra* (see page 152). Very surprised, a Japanese chef came and asked me where I had got to know this 'Japanese ingredient'. Frequently we take possession of ingredients without knowing their history or origin.

In Brazil, okra is often despised. But it also has passionate fans who, sword in hand, are always ready to defend it. I don't need to tell you which side I am on. The dish I call *okra, okra, okra* is an ode to this cultural paradox.

The reason for the prejudice is the vegetable's high cellulose content: once cooked, it oozes a mucus that gives it a slippery texture. But okra goes well beyond this. As with all ingredients, deciding how to handle them is up to the chef: fried; roasted; using its mucus to thicken a broth or simply to make edible paper. This is the idea behind the recipe. Okra seeds, cooked with care, become a kind of delicate earth caviar which explodes in the mouth and delights the diner with its flavour.

Okra, okra, okra

SERVES 4

	Ingredients	Preparation
Toasted vegetable stock (stage 1)	• **1 head garlic** • **2 each red, yellow and green bell peppers, deseeded and quartered** • **3 medium tomatoes, halved** • **3 medium onions, peeled and halved** • **rapeseed (canola) oil (for coating the vegetables)** • **1 bunch thyme** • **1 bunch rosemary** • **8 black peppercorns**	• Preheat the oven to 180°C/355°F. • Place the garlic on a baking sheet and roast in the oven for 30 minutes. When cool, cut in half and set aside. • Place all the vegetables in a large bowl and mix with a few drops of rapeseed (canola) oil. • Heat the grill (broiler) to a high heat. Place the vegetables on a rack and grill (broil) on both sides. • Place the grilled vegetables in a vacuum bag with the garlic, thyme, rosemary, peppercorns and 300 ml water. • Cook in a sous vide at 60°C/140°F for 3 hours. • Strain the contents of the bag into a bowl through a sieve (strainer) lined with a closely woven muslin cloth. Set the stock aside.
Okra roe	• **500 g okra** • **1 small onion, halved and finely sliced** • **olive oil** • **salt** • **black pepper** • **rapeseed (canola) oil (for frying/sweating)** • **6 drops Jerez vinegar**	• Cut 200 g of the okra into rings and set aside. • Cut the ends off 200 g of the remaining okra, remove the seeds and discard the rest. • Bring a medium pan of salted water to the boil and cook the okra seeds for 4 minutes, then drain. • Place in a bowl and mix in 50ml of the toasted vegetable stock. • Cut the remaining 100g okra vertically into thin strips. • Place some oil in a small pan over low heat, add the sliced onion, cover and cook until transparent. • Place a few drops of rapeseed (canola) oil in a pan, add the okra rings and toast them over medium heat. • Add the fried onions, salt, pepper and Jerez vinegar, mix gently together and set aside to keep warm. • Heat some rapeseed (canola) oil in a frying pan or skillet over high heat and fry the strips of okra in the hot oil until golden. • Remove the okra seeds from the stock, drain and set aside.
Okra paper	• **150 g okra** • **1 fresh hot chilli pepper, finely chopped** • **15 g glucose** • **salt**	• Preheat the oven to 90°C/195°F. • Bring a pan of water to the boil and blanch the okra for 2 minutes. • Strain and place the okra in the jug of a blender with the chilli, glucose and a pinch of salt and blend until smooth. • Pour the mixture onto a Silpat and place in the oven for 30 minutes. • Remove from the oven and turn up the heat to 120°C/250°F. • Cut the okra 'paper' into irregular squares. Crumple some aluminium foil into a loose ball and place on a baking sheet. Lay the okra 'paper' shapes over it. • Return to the oven at 120°C/250°F for 1 minute until crispy. Remove from the oven and place on a rack so they remain crisp.
Baked okra	• **olive oil** • **Salt**	• Preheat the heat to 180°C/355°F. • Put the okra on a baking sheet, drizzle with olive oil and sprinkle over some salt. • Place in the oven, bake for 5 minutes, remove and keep warm.
Toasted vegetable stock (stage 2)	• **2 parsley leaves** • **2 basil leaves** • **6 rosemary leaves** • **1 bunch thyme** • **4 gelatine leaves** • **salt and black pepper**	• Warm the toasted vegetable stock to 50°C/120°F. • Rehydrate the gelatine leaves in a small bowl of cold water. • Add the herbs to the stock and infuse for 1 minute. • Strain the stock into a warmed container and season with salt. • Add the rehydrated gelatine leaves to the stock and keep warm.

Finish and Presentation

• Place one spoonful of sautéed okra in the centre of a deep serving dish.
• Place a small serving of the okra 'roe' on top and garnish with some fried okra, some of the baked okra and a few pieces of okra 'paper'.
• Finish with a little of the toasted vegetable stock poured around the vegetables.

152

Heart of palm

There has always been a strong tradition of eating palm hearts in Brazil, particularly the varieties sold in cans. The reason for canning the palm and not using it fresh is due to the fact that until the 1980s the species that was most commonly used tended to oxidize quickly, become dark and unappealing in a very short time. This was the *juçara* palm, a species endemic to the Atlantic jungle. The harvesting of this palm was so invasive that the species became endangered and it became imperative to find a sustainable variety to protect the *juçara* and support the demand for palm hearts.

Today, the variety that is used is *pupunha* or beach palm which is native to the Amazon forest. The main reason we use this variety is environmental. The *juçara* variety takes up to eight years to produce 700 grams of heart and, after the heart is extracted, the tree dies. *Pupunha* is different. Each plant from this species forms a cluster of stems. From each of those stems two kilograms of palm heart can be extracted and this extraction can be managed in a way that ensures that the plant does not die. It also takes considerably less time to grow and can be harvested after only two years. Another advantage of *pupunha* is that is does not darken, so it can be used raw.

With the use of *pupunha*, we widen the possibilities of the heart of palm. In the restaurant, it is served raw, roasted, boiled or made into fettucine, something we are known for.

Heart of palm brandade with anchovies from Cantábrico

SERVES 4

| | Ingredients | Preparation | Finish and Presentation |

Heart of palm brandade

Ingredients
- 1 Pupunha heart of palm (see page 154)
- 125 g butter

Preparation
- Preheat the oven to 200°C/400°F.
- Wrap the heart of palm in aluminium foil, place on a baking sheet and bake for 60 minutes.
- Remove from the oven and turn the heat down to 180°C/355°F.
- Take the heart of palm out of the foil, put back on the baking sheet then return to the oven for a further 60 minutes or until tender.
- Cut the heart of palm in half and scoop out the pulp into a bowl.
- Mash the pulp with a fork .
- Place the mashed heart of palm pulp in a bowl with a little of the butter and beat with a whisk.
- Add the rest of the butter, a little at a time, whisking constantly until creamy.

Finish and Presentation
- **50 ml demi-glace**
- **4 fillets of Cantabrian anchovy in oil**

- In a small pan over low heat, warm the demi-glace.
- Make a quenelle of brandade and place it on the plate.
- Arrange one anchovy fillet over the quenelle and drizzle a little of its own oil over it.
- Drizzle thin stripes of demi-glace over the dish.

Fresh heart of palm with scallops

SERVES 4

	Ingredients	Preparation	Finish and Presentation
Herb oil	• **15 g parsley** • **5 g sage** • **5 g thyme** • **5 g oregano** • **5 g rosemary** • **250 ml extra virgin olive oil**	• Chop the herbs and mix with the oil in a bowl. Set aside.	• **10 g grated horseradish** • **sea salt** • Place one disc of heart of palm on the plate, then place half a scallop on it and a small spoonful of horseradish on top. Continue to build the dish with another heart of palm disc then another half a scallop and some horseradish. Repeat this twice, ending with the scallop.
Basil oil	• **50 g (1¾ oz) fresh basil** • **50 ml (2 fl oz) rapeseed (canola) oil**	• Bring a pan of water to the boil, remove from the heat and place the basil leaves in it. Leave for 5 seconds. • Drain the leaves and place them quickly in ice-cold water. • Drain again and fold them in a clean dish towel, then lightly twist to remove the excess water. • Using a blender, mix the leaves and oil together for about a minute. • Place the mixture in a small pan and heat it (do not let the temperature rise above 65°C/150°F for ten minutes. • Remove from the heat, allow to cool and then sieve (strain) through a fine chinois.	• Place a garnish of seasoned squid on top and sprinkle a little sea salt over the composition. • On a slate, make a trace of coral sauce, adding a dash of basil oil on top. Place the heart of palm composition at the other end of the slate. Finish with the chervil.
Coral sauce	• **50 ml (2 fl oz) lime juice** • **25 ml (1 fl oz) soy sauce** • **corals from 8 scallops**	• Remove the brown parts from the corals. • Using a blender, mix together the lime juice, the soy sauce and the corals. • Strain through a chinois and set aside in the refrigerator.	
Fresh heart of palm with scallops	• **120 g squid (cleaned)** • **20 g hijiki seaweed** • **10 ml herb oil (above)** • **chopped chives** • **chopped parsley** • **8 scallops** • **200 g pupunha heart of palm (see page 154)** • **coral sauce** • **10 ml basil oil** • **chervil** • **salt and pepper**	• Bring a large pan of water to the boil. Have ready a bowl of water with ice. • Cut the squid in fine rings and blanch them in the boiling water for about two seconds, then immerse them immediately in the ice water, so that the thermal shock stops the cooking. Drain and set aside. • Rehydrate the hijiki seaweed in cold water for two minutes. • Drain and mix the seaweed with the squid rings. Season them with the herb oil, chives, parsley, salt and pepper. • Cut the scallops in two parts. • Using a mandoline, cut the heart of palm in 2-mm slices. Use a 4-cm round metal ring to cut out discs from the heart of palm slices.	

Heart of palm fettuccine carbonara

SERVES 4

Ingredients

Heart of palm fettuccine
- 1 kg heart of palm

Carbonara sauce
- 100 g bacon
- 10 egg yolks, sieved
- 160 g Grana Padano
- 80 ml bacon fat
- 200 ml double (heavy) cream

Preparation

- Remove the bark from the heart of palm.
- Using a mandoline, cut the heart of palm lengthwise. Weigh out 4 portions of 130 g each and set aside.

- Cut the bacon into small cubes.
- Heat a frying pan over low heat and add the bacon cubes. Fry until the crispy and well coloured.
- Take the bacon out of the pan and place on a paper towel. Reserve the bacon fat.
- In a large bowl mix the egg yolks with the Grana Padano, then add the bacon fat and lastly stir in the cream.

Finish and Presentation

- **5 g chives, finely chopped**
- **salt and pepper**

- Bring a large pan of salted water to the boil and cook the heart of palm fettuccine until al dente.
- Warm a large frying pan or skillet over medium heat then place the cooked fettuccine in the pan.
- Mix the carbonara sauce into the fettuccine and adjust the seasoning.
- Keep stirring, working briskly and thoroughly through all the contents of the pan so the sauce thickens rapidly and becomes smooth and glossy (do not let the yolks overcook).
- Place a serving of the fettucine in their sauce in the bottom of a deep dish.
- Scatter some of the bacon cubes over the fettucine.
- Finish with a grinding of black pepper and a few chopped chives.

Heart of palm fettuccine with prawns

SERVES 4

	Ingredients	Preparation	Finish and Presentation
Coral butter	• 30 ml olive oil • 3 cloves garlic, finely chopped • 500g prawn (shrimp) heads • 400 g butter	• Place the oil in a large frying pan or skillet and fry the garlic briefly without browning. • Add the shrimps' heads and mix well, pressing the heads with a wooden spoon to release the coral. Continue this process for 5 minutes. • Transfer the shrimp mixture to a large pan, add 300 ml water and mix thoroughly, then cook over low heat for approximately 20 minutes. • Remove from the heat and when cool add the butter. • Place in a blender and process to a smooth and uniform mixture. Set aside.	• Place a serving of the heart of palm fettuccine in the centre of the dish and arrange the grilled prawns (shrimp) over it.
Heart of palm fettuccine	• 1 kg heart of palm • 12 prawns (shrimp) • olive oil, for pan frying • coral butter (above) • salt and pepper	• Remove the bark from the heart of palm. • Using a mandoline, cut the heart of palm into fine strips, so that it resembles fettuccine. • Bring a large pan of salted water to the boil, carefully add the fettuccine strips and blanch for one minute. Drain and set aside. • Season the prawns (shrimp) with salt and pepper. • Heat a little oil in a medium frying pan or skillet and grill the shrimps until golden. • Place the coral butter in a large frying pan or skillet and melt over low heat. • Add the fettuccine to the coral butter and season to taste. • Cook for about 3 minutes mixing all the time over low heat until the sauce reaches a creamy consistency.	

Corn

Until the 1500s, corn (maize) was restricted to the Americas. From the Andes to Argentina, different varieties prospered here. Thus, Italian polenta has the American continent in its DNA. Its recipe is attributed to the Guarani tribespeople, who had corn as their staple food. The Guarani are also, according to anthropologists, one of the few South American ethnic groups that practised agriculture before colonization. Dried corn, ground in a rustic way and then cooked, acquires a unique flavour and texture. In a fit of patriotism, I would say it is even more interesting than polenta.

Popcorn has always enchanted us: there is no Brazilian home with children where popcorn is not eaten. What fascinated me the most when I ate it was the grains that did not pop, which were darker and hard on the teeth, but had a stronger flavour. With this flavour in my personal register, I searched for a type of corn that did not pop. I found it. I fried it. I ground it. In this book, I use a popcorn powder (see page 166) that is not simply ground popcorn. It has impressive flavour and potency.

Heart of palm fettuccine with butter, sage, Parmesan cheese and popcorn powder

SERVES 4

	Ingredients	Preparation	Finish and Presentation
Popcorn powder	• rapeseed (canola) oil • 100 g broken corn (quirera) • salt	• In a large frying pan or skillet heat the oil until it reaches 180°C/350°F. • Fry the broken corn in batches until it opens like popcorn. • Spread it over a sheet of kitchen towel and leave to cool. • Process the corn until it turns to powder. • Sift twice through a fine sieve (strainer) and season with salt. Set aside.	• 1 small courgette (zucchini) • 60 g unsalted butter • 15 sage leaves • 50 g Parmesan cheese, finely shaved • salt and pepper
Clarified butter	• 10 ml unsalted butter	• In a small pan melt the butter over low heat for about 45 minutes, constantly skimming to remove the impurities. • Strain twice through a fine sieve lined with muslin (cheesecloth) and reserve in a small bowl.	• Cut the courgette (zucchini) into fine roundels. • Heat a frying pan or skillet, add the clarified butter and seal the roundels on one side. • Heat the unsalted butter until it turns slightly brown and foamy.
Heart of palm fettucine	• 1 kg heart of palm	• Peel the bark from the heart of palm. • Using a mandoline, cut the heart of palm in fine strips so that it resembles fettuccine. • Bring a large pan of salted water to the boil, carefully drop in the fettuccine strips and blanch for one minute.	• Add the sage and then the blanched strips of heart of palm. Correct the seasoning. • Pile a serving of the heart of palm fettuccine in the centre of a dish, arranging the zucchini on one side and a shaving of Parmesan cheese on the other. • Garnish with a sprinkling of the popcorn powder.

Amazonian herbs

Cooking has given me the opportunity to travel around the world and make discoveries. For a curious expedition lover, this has been without a doubt the biggest personal gain from my profession. Some destinations are recurring in a chef's imagination. Japan, China and Thailand have always intrigued me for their unique ways of producing flavour. In these places, the simple, the potent and the tenuous walk side-by-side in unexpected ways.

Going to Thailand has improved my understanding of aromatic potency: the strength and rusticity of chillies; the seduction of herbs; the hot; the tepid; the liquid. After swimming for a while in that environment, I understood a few things that I knew, but did not know I knew. Let me explain: Brazil's tucupi, liquid, tepid, aromatic, hot, carries within it the hot, humid, frenetic environment of an Amazonian city. On the other side of the planet I found similarities to, and coincidences with, the largest cities of the Amazon: Manaus and Belém. When one speaks of the inhabitants of the Amazon, one tends to think only of its tribespeople, but when I visited Bangkok I realized that both Manaus and Belém also happen to have more than 2 million inhabitants, and they deal with herbs, broths and fermented liquids in a very similar way. Thai cuisine is rich in broths, as is that of the Amazon. The biggest star is, again, tucupi (see page 198). It is elegant, fermented, pungent and complex. All along the Brazilian coast, as in Thailand, we find fish stews, starting with *moquecas* in the south, going up through *caldeiradas* and ending in the north with *mujecas* and *quinhampiras*. The difference between them is in the amount of water used in their preparation. Regional variations in the ingredients again remind one of Thai cuisine in the aromatic notes. Visiting Thailand has helped me understand better what I have here in Brazil.

Here is a little more detail about the herbs from the Amazon:

Culantro is a wild coriander (cilantro), of untamed character, that reminds me of the beauty and energy of a wild horse. Its aroma is similar to that of coriander – which comes from the Latin coriandro and means, in free translation, stinkbug odour. It reinforces our fascination with bad, weird things. This fear-cum-tolerance can, with time and persistence, lead to passion.

Amazonian wild basil is a member of the extensive and complex basilicum family. It carries a poignant and simple note.

Pimenta de cheiro (aromatic chili pepper), one of the aromatic elements that fascinate me the most in Brazilian cuisine. Even though it is from the family of chilli peppers, it is not hot, but has an uncommon, potent aroma, full of character.

Cariru is typically Amazonian, but still undervalued. It has a distinctive texture, with a strong acidic note.

Roselle is not native to Brazil, but it is here that we started using its leaves in recipes. In Japan, where it originates, cooks use only its flowers. Its main characteristic, as its Portuguese name of *vinagreira* indicates, is its strong acidity.

Guineafowl with herb ravioli

SERVES 4

	Ingredients	Preparation	Finish and presentation
Broth	• **2 guineafowls** • **4 tomatoes** • **1 onion** • **3 cloves garlic** • **1 celery stick** • **1 small leek** • **1 bay leaf** • **10 g chopped parsley** • **10 g chopped cilantro (coriander)** • **100 ml white wine**	• Separate the thighs and the breasts from the guineafowls, reserving the carcasses. • Place the tomatoes, onion, garlic, celery, leek, leaf and guineafowl carcasses in a large pan over a low heat and leave to stew. • Add the white wine, parsley and coriander (cilantro) and leave to cook over low heat until the liquid has reduced by half. • Strain and reserve.	• **mushroom blades and edible flowers, to garnish** • **sea salt** • Preheat the oven to 180°C/355°F. • Cook the guineafowl in the oven for 10–12 minutes, until golden and with a crispy skin. • Heat the broth in a medium pan over a gentle heat until just simmering.
Guinea-fowl	• **Breasts and thighs from the guineafowls (above)** • **1 sprig rosemary** • **2 sprigs thyme** • **200 ml white wine** • **salt and pepper**	• Place the the thighs and breasts of the guineafowl in a bowl and season with salt and pepper, add the rosemary, thyme and white wine to the bowl and leave to marinate for eight hours. • Transfer the mixture to a vacuum bag and cook in a sous vide for 6 hours at 60°C/140°F. • Remove from the vacuum bag and set aside to cool.	• Add the ravioli to the broth and cook for 30 seconds. • Place a portion of the guineafowl in the centre of a wide bowl. • Set a herb ravioli beside the guineafowl. • Spoon a little of the broth over the dish.
Herb ravioli	• **200 g heart of palm** • **20 g arrowleaf elephant ear, chopped** • **20 g ora pro nóbis** • **10 g aromatic pepper, chopped**	• Cut the heart of palm into very thin slices using a mandolin. • On a cutting board, place one slice of the heart of palm horizontally and another slice across the first vertically. • Place a portion of the herbs and aromatic pepper in the centre. • Fold closed like a ravioli and set aside. • Repeat until all of the ingredients are used up.	• Garnish with mushroom blades, edible flowers and a sprinkling of sea salt.

Jambu

I go to the Amazon frequently. On these expeditions I rarely know what I am looking for, but I always know what I find. And these discoveries drive me to new expeditions. It was on one of those trips that I found one of the most intriguing herbs of the Amazon, jambu, from the paracress family, which produces a fascinating sensation in the mouth like electricity. On the island of Mauritius in the Indian ocean is a related plant that provokes a similar sensation. Brazilian jambu creates some confusion, a short circuit in our taste buds. The buds of the plant are known as Szechuan buttons and are used in the Green tomato gel recipe on page 174.

I have been reading, going to lectures and carrying out research for some time in order to understand what is known in Japanese cuisine as the fifth flavour – umami or savoury, the other four being sweet, sour, bitter and salty. It is what Parmesan cheese, cured ham, mushrooms, soy sauce and some algae have in common. In a still very empirical way, I believe I have found its equivalent in Brazilian ingredients. The combination of fermented tucupi with the typical herbs from the Amazon – coriander, wild basil and aromatic chilli – form an Amazonian umami, which is made more potent by this confusion on the tip of the tongue, this tremor, which is how the tribespeople describe the sensation produced by jambu. This broth brings us a sensation of pleasure, common to the ingredients described as umami.

Green tomato gel

SERVES 4

Ingredients

Green tomato gel

- 20 green tomatoes
- 15 ml white vinegar
- 8 g salt
- 8 g gelatine sheets

Preparation

- Using a centrifuge, remove the juice of the tomatoes and strain it into a bowl through a fine chinois lined with a wet cloth.
- Season with vinegar and salt.
- In a shallow dish, hydrate the gelatine sheets with ice-cold water.
- Using a cooking thermometer, heat ⅓ of the tomato juice to 60°C/140°F and add the gelatine, then the rest of the juice.
- Place 3 small ladlefuls of the mixture in the bottom of each of the serving plates, and place them in the refrigerator for 2 hours.

Finish and presentation

- 5 ml extra virgin olive oil
- 4 g black salt
- 4 g coriander seeds, lightly crushed
- 1 orange supreme, the segments divided into 3 parts
- basil leaves
- fine salt
- the seeds of one red tomato
- 4 cobs Peruvian corn, toasted
- jambu/ sechuan buttons
- beetroot sprouts
- chervil sprouts
- celery sprouts
- clover leaves
- watercress sprouts
- purslane
- edible flowers, such as borage

- Take the plates from the refrigerator and drizzle the olive oil over the gel, then sprinkle black salt and coriander seeds over the surface.
- Arrange the orange supreme segments on the surface of the gel and garnish with the basil leaves, then sprinkle a touch of fine salt over each piece of orange supreme.
- Place the tomato seeds alongside the coriander seeds.
- Finish with the Peruvian corn kernels, the sechuan buttons, the sprouts and the flowers.

Brazilian mushroom

For more than a decade I've been searching for proof of the existence of native mushrooms in Brazil and just days before this book goes to print I have received them at the D.O.M. for the first time.

Nature has always been the greatest inspiration for everything I do. I am lucky enough to have been a boy from a simple family, passionate about hunting and fishing. On family expeditions, with little money and limited means of travel to remote places, I could get to know, try and enjoy genuine, authentic flavours, always in my grandfather's or my father's company. Brazilian flavours were present inside me long before I started cooking. On each trip, a flavour; on each trip, a memory; on each trip, a mental photograph. During the years that I lived in Europe, I got acquainted with other flavours, other landscapes and other memories. It was in Europe that I developed the habit of summing up each forest and wood in terms of its herbs, mushrooms and nuts. To do the same with the Amazon rainforest took some time.

It was easy enough to sum up the forest by its herbs and nuts, but the mushrooms were missing. What we do have is tucupi, a fermented liquid deriving from cassava. Fermentation in the Amazon is almost spontaneous – it is present at every moment. It is common when arriving at the Amazon to feel a slightly humid, acidic note that invades one's body: it is not an environment for the germination of mushrooms. From this line of reasoning one of our dishes was born: Mushroom consommé with herbs from the forest and garden (page 178). It was a dish that suggested a leap over the Atlantic, from the woods of Europe to the rainforest of South America. With each spoonful, a flavour; with each spoonful, a point of union; with each spoonful, the greatest expression of nature.

The confirmation of the existence of Brazilian mushrooms came from the city of Manaus, Amazonas. A young chef, Felipe Schaedler, sent me a study by two researchers from INPA (an institute of botanic research) who confirmed that there are indigenous communities eating mushrooms in Brazil. For years I have been talking to people – researchers, botanists, scientists – begging for crumbs of information about native mushrooms. They existed, I was sure – reports from caboclos and ethnic groups from many regions supported this and there is an important tradition of harvesting and eating them in the neighbouring country of Argentina. Now I have proof that Brazilian mushrooms exist, but there is still much to discover.

In the south of Brazil, there are mentions of mushrooms and other reports come from the countryside of Minas Gerais. In the highlands of Rio Negro, there are reports of a tribe that cultivates a species of mushroom and treats it as a delicacy. There is a ritual involved in its cultivation. The tribespeople cut a tree with a black trunk called *pixuna*, which means 'black' in the native language. They marinate it and smoke it, then wait for up to six months. At some point, for a reason that we still don't know or understand, mushrooms flourish. We need to study this process and document it scientifically.

Mushroom consommé with herbs from the forest and garden

SERVES 4

Ingredients

Shiitake consommé
- 200 g dried shiitake mushrooms
- 1 litre water
- 30 ml white wine vinegar

Garlic oil
- 50 g peeled garlic
- 100 ml olive oil

Mushroom sauté with forest herbs
- 30 g shimeji mushrooms
- 30 g shiitake mushrooms
- 30 g button mushrooms
- garlic oil
- 10 g basil
- 10 g sawtooth coriander
- 10 g jambu/ sechuan button
- 10 g cariru
- herb oil

Preparation

- Chop the dried shiitake mushrooms roughly and place them in a pan with the water and vinegar.
- Bring to simmering point then simmer over low heat for about 40 minutes.
- Remove from the heat and cool.
- Drain the mushrooms and set aside, reserving the liquid.

- Place the garlic and the oil in a blender and blend thoroughly.
- Decant into a covered container and set aside in the fridge.

- Cut the mushrooms into fine slivers, reserving some whole for the decoration.
- Heat a frying pan or skillet and add a dash of garlic oil.
- Sauté the chopped mushrooms.
- Remove from the heat and add the chopped forest herbs and the herb oil.

Finish and Presentation

- chives
- chervil
- curly parsley
- basil
- parsley
- beetroot sprouts
- clover sprouts
- purslane
- sechuan button flowers
- edible flowers
- pepper

- Place a serving of the mushroom sauté in a soup plate and garnish it with the garden herbs and the raw mushrooms.
- Grind some fresh black pepper over it.
- Pour the hot consommé into a heated jug and serve beside the soup plate.

Mushroom with smoked parsnips

SERVES 4

	Ingredients	Preparation	Finish and Presentation
Parsnips and mushrooms	• **1 kg coarse salt** • **300 g parsnip, washed** • **150 g fresh button mushrooms**	• Preheat the oven to 200°C. • Dampen the coarse salt. • Place half the salt on the bottom of a roasting pan. • Place the parsnips on top of the salt in a single layer. • Cover the parsnips with the rest of the coarse salt. • Bake for one hour. • Remove from the oven and transfer the parsnips to a rack to cool. • When cool, peel the skin off the parsnips and cut them into 4 pieces lengthwise. Set aside. • In a large dry frying pan or skillet toast the button mushrooms directly over flame until golden brown. Set aside and keep warm.	• **extra virgin olive oil, for coating the parsnips and for the presentation** • **smoked salt** • **4 black garlic cloves** • **parsley, chopped** • **salt** • **pepper** • Place the parsnips in a clean roasting pan and coat lightly with olive oil. • Return the parsnips to the oven for about 3 minutes to warm through. • Remove from the oven and season with the smoked salt. • Season the mushrooms with salt and pepper and place a mound of them in the centre of a dish. • Cut the cloves of black garlic in half. • Arrange 2 pieces of parsnip and 2 halves of black garlic beside the mushrooms. • Finish with a drizzle of olive oil and a sprinkling of parsley.

Erva mate

When we Brazilians think about the south of the country, the theme is always *churrasco*, or barbecue, the gaucho tradition from Brazil, Uruguay, Paraguay and Argentina of grilling meat on charcoal embers.

Around the barbecue, there is another strong cultural habit: drinking erva mate or *chimarrão*, as we call it in Brazil. Normally one puts the herb in a gourd, adding hot water before drinking the infusion through a straw, called a bomba. Gauchos drink erva mate through the day, a habit that is similar to the drinking of espresso coffee or tea elsewhere in the world.

A few years ago, one of my chefs participated in a competition to represent gaucho cuisine in one dish. He asked for my help and I remembered the flavour triad that I had learned from Ferran Adrià, and tried to transport it to the south of my country. Suddenly, it became clear: barbecue, yerba mate and sweet potato, a combination so common in that region. It is traditional there to throw sweet potatoes into the ashes of the barbecue, so that they can be slowly roasted and eaten with the meat. Erva mate permeates the whole ritual. I had there all the information that I needed: ashes, coals, smoke. A piece of meat, a type of herb to make an infusion and a tuberous root. I consulted the classical sources. How does one prepare a good meat dish in Europe? French cuisine came to mind, and I thought about a good steak, which, for a Frenchman, must be served with a sauce béarnaise, in which we would replace the tarragon with erva mate.

In our first attempt, the béarnaise was satisfactory, the potatoes were great, and the meat was sensational. But the combination was disastrous. Nevertheless we did not accept defeat. We persisted and ended up with the recipe on page 184: Sweet potato roasted in a salt crust, with an onion coal and the erva mate béarnaise.

PS: my chef got second place.

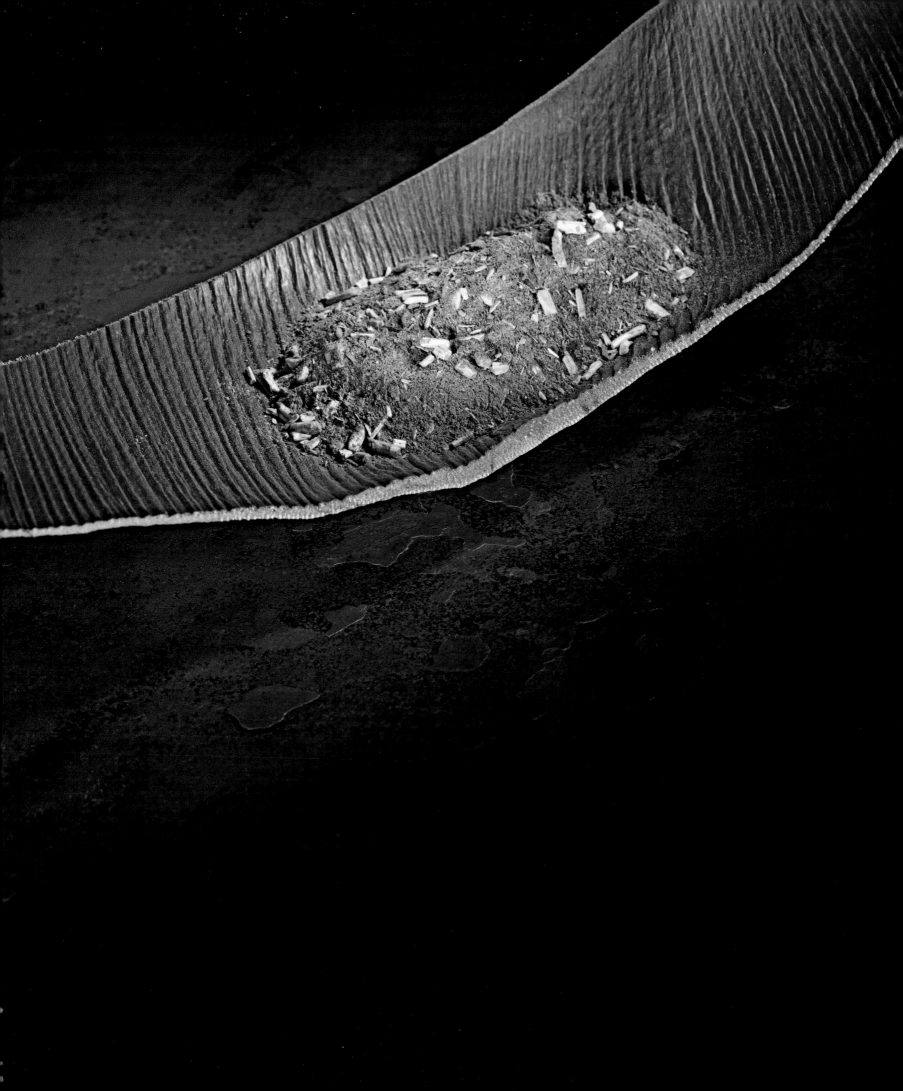

Sweet Potato with erva mate béarnaise

SERVES 4

	Ingredients	Preparation	Finish and presentation
Sweet potato	• **4 white sweet potatoes** • **1 kg coarse salt** • **water for sprinkling**	• Preheat the oven to 200°C/400°F. • Scrub the potatoes, then place them on a baking sheet and fully cover with coarse salt. Sprinkle water over the salt and bake in the oven for 1 hour. • Leave the potatoes to cool down completely in the salt. • Lift off the caked salt and discard. Wipe the potatoes using paper towels.	• **black salt** • **chives** • Warm the potatoes and cut them in slices. • On a slate, make a trace with the béarnaise, lay a slice of the sweet potato on it and garnish with black salt and chives.
Erva mate reduction	• **50 g erva mate tea** • **100 ml white vinegar** • **100 ml white wine** • **1 white onion** • **1 leaf laurel** • **1 sprig rosemary** • **1 sprig thyme**	• In a medium size pan mix all the ingredients and simmer over low heat for 30 minutes. • Strain through a fine sieve (strainer) lined with a very clean cloth.	
Aromatic clarified butter	• **250 g of butter** • **25 g of erva mate tea, brewed**	• Place the butter and the brewed erva mate tea in a small pan and simmer over low heat for 10 minutes. • Strain through a fine sieve (strainer) lined with a very clean cloth.	
Erva mate béarnaise sauce	• **4 egg yolks** • **erva mate reduction (above)** • **aromatic clarified butter (above)**	• In a bowl placed in a bain marie, heat the egg yolks gently, stirring constantly. • Add the erva mate reduction and beat with a hand whisk, then add the aromatic clarified butter slowly, beating until the mixture emulsifies and becomes creamy.	

Priprioca

Diving even deeper in the universe of the roots, I arrive at priprioca. Traditionally used to make perfume, it is an aromatic element which I use a lot in my kitchen. I take pride in having developed the gastronomic use of this root after discovering that it was not toxic, together with an important fragrance business. Native to the Amazon, priprioca is as versatile as vanilla but with very different flavour nuances – slightly earthy, with wood and charcoal notes – which can bring new sensations to many food products. Priprioca essence may be added to a great number of recipes, and it significantly alters the aroma of the dishes and the experience of the eater. Sustainable use of priprioca can also bring social and economic benefits to the inhabitants of the Amazon region, which makes me believe that, through doing the right thing with an ingredient, I can make a positive change in the environment.

Chilled beetroot cream, mandarin, priprioca and cold squid

SERVES 4

	Ingredients	**Preparation**	**Finish and Presentation**
Beetroot cream	• **400 g beetroot, peeled** • **100 ml concentrated mandarin juice** • **60 ml water** • **30 ml olive oil** • **10 ml priprioca essence** • **salt** • **pepper** • **Tabasco**	• Slice the beetroot thinly. • Place the beetroot, mandarin juice, water, olive oil and priprioca essence in a vacuum bag and cook in the sous-vide for five hours at 85°C. • Transfer the contents to the Thermomix and combine to a smooth, even cream. • Season to taste.	• **150 g wakame, rehydrated** • **50 g spring onion (scallion)** • Slice the spring onion (scallion) down the middle then slice it into thin strips approximately 0.2 mm wide. • Place the spring onion strips in a bowl of water and ice, so that they curl slightly. Drain thoroughly. • Place a serving of the beetroot cream in the middle of a dish and garnish with the cold squid, the wakame and the spring strips.
Cold squid	• **90 g coarse salt** • **900 g ice** • **4 litres water** • **500 g baby squid, cleaned**	• Into a container with a tightly fitting lid place 30g of the salt, 300g of the ice, 1 litre of the water and the squid. • Replace the lid and shake the container vigorously for about five minutes or until a thick foam forms. Repeat this operation three more times. • Then shake the squid again with the remaining ice and water for 10 more minutes. • Leave the squid in a bowl of fresh water and ice until ready to serve.	

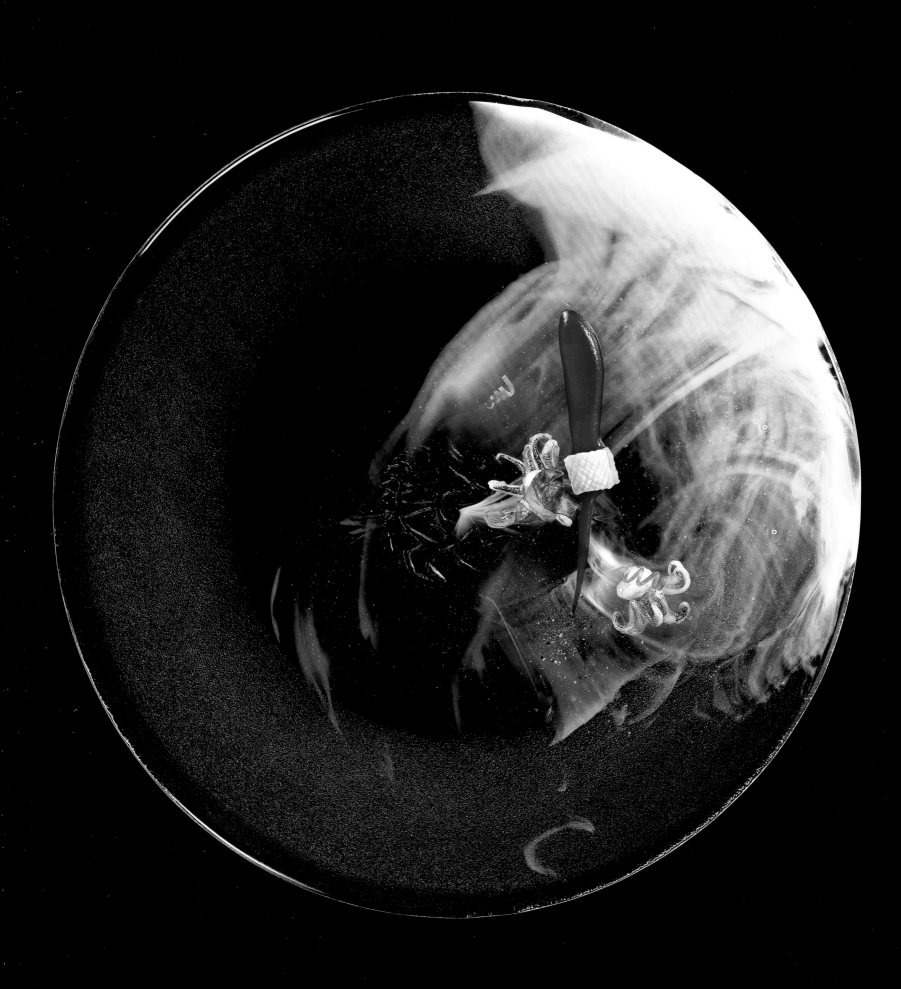

Manioc

If I had to choose a symbol to represent Brazilian cuisine, it would not be caipirinha, nor rice and beans, but manioc, also known as cassava. From north to south, from east to west, the 200 million or so inhabitants of Brazil use the flour made from this tuberous root in their meals. A fundamental element of the diet of the indigenous people who lived here before the Portuguese arrived, there are more than 250 species of manioc. Its three main subproducts are: manioc flour, tapioca and tucupi.

Manioc flour is manioc pulp that has been grated, pressed and then toasted. The type (or types) of manioc, the coarseness of the grater, the degree to which it is toasted, the way or ways in which even the same type of manioc has been prepared – raw or fermented, for example – result in an infinite variety of flours. There are also crunchy, fine or even hard textures. Flavour notes also vary from raw via toasted to lightly burnt. When flour is added to fermented manioc it produces yet another type of flour, which has an acidity similar to that of bread made with natural yeast.

Farofa is a dish containing manioc flour plus some sort of fat and other ingredients. There are endless variations: with fruit, with dried meats, with smoked ingredients, with preserves such as olives and capers. Textures are also countless: moist, dry, crunchy, smooth. The first sensation that a foreigner experiences when tasting a farofa is one of strangeness. Dry, sandy and unusual to those who are not familiar with Brazilian culture, manioc flours and farofas do not create a great first impression. But with time these same people request the recipe and go from strangeness to tolerance and from tolerance to fascination. Manioc flours and farofas may have something addictive about them, which I understood a few years ago when modern chefs started making earths and crunchies to put into recipes. I had already been making these for some time, and my faith and pride in them increased when fellow chefs shared the idea.

Baby pork ribs in Malbec and Brás manioc

SERVES 4

	Ingredients	Preparation	Finish and Presentation
Baby pork ribs	• 800 g baby pork ribs • 2 onions • 3 garlic cloves • 2 carrots • 1 fresh hot chilli pepper • 2 sprigs parsley • 1 sprig peppermint • 50 ml white wine vinegar • 6 tomatoes • 300 ml white wine • rapeseed (canola) oil • 1 bay leaf • Salt and pepper	• Cut the ribs into sections allowing two bones per portion. Set aside. • Chop the onions, garlic, carrots and chilli pepper into small pieces. Set aside. • Chop the peppermint and parsley roughly. Set aside. • Season the ribs with salt and pepper and place in a large bowl with the herbs, the vinegar and the chopped vegetables, cover and marinate in the refrigerator for 24 hours. • After this period, remove the meat from the marinade. Strain the vegetables and sprigs of herbs from the marinade and set aside. • Heat a dash of oil in a frying pan or skillet and fry the meat until golden on both sides then add the vegetables, the tomatoes and the bay leaf. Sauté for ten minutes. • Add the wine and allow it to evaporate then add the herbs, cover with water and simmer for 4 hours, or until the meat is tender. Remove the meat and set aside. • Sieve the broth and return to a large clean pan to reduce over low heat until it has halved in quantity. Cover and set aside.	• To reheat the ribs, brush them with the glaze and place in a roasting pan. • Place in the oven at 200ºC/400ºF for 30 seconds. Repeat the whole process twice more. • In a bowl, mix the fried manioc and the mayonnaise, the caramelized onion and the chopped parsley. Season with salt and pepper. • Place a serving of the manioc at the centre of the dish. • Arrange the ribs over the manioc and spoon some of the foam around the side of the ribs.
Honey and spice glaze	• 100 ml honey • 100 ml beef broth • 50 ml white wine vinegar • 10 g coriander seeds • 10 g cinnamon sticks • 5 g clove • 5 g black peppercorns • 1 star anise • 5 g allspice • 1 fresh hot chilli pepper	• Place all the ingredients in a medium sized pan and simmer over low heat until reduced to half its volume. Do not allow to boil. Sieve (strain) and set aside.	
Brás manioc	• 500 g peeled manioc • 1 litre rapeseed (canola) oil, plus extra for caramelizing the onion • 2 egg yolks • 100 ml extra virgin olive oil • 10 ml Jerez vinegar • •1 onion • 1 sprig parsley • salt and black pepper	• With the aid of a mandoline, cut the manioc in matchstick strips. • Heat the oil in a deep fryer to a temperature of 180°C/350°F. • Bring a large pan of salted water to the boil and when the oil is at the right temperature, blanch the manioc strips in the water for one minute, then drain well and fry immediately in the oil until crispy. Strain and dry well with kitchen towel. • Make a mayonnaise with the yolks and the olive oil. Add the vinegar and season with salt. Set aside. • Cut the onions in half-moon slices. • Heat a dash of oil in a frying pan or skillet and caramelize the onion slices over low heat. Set aside. • Chop the parsley roughly and set aside.	
Malbec foam	• 200 ml of the broth from the cooked ribs' • 100 ml reduced Malbec wine • 25 g unsalted butter • 10 g soy lecithin • salt	• Place the broth in a medium sized pan with the wine and heat to a temperature of 60°C/140°F. • Remove from the heat and using an electric mixer, incorporate the soy lecithin until it foams. • Correct the seasoning and set aside.	

Tapioca

In the process of working manioc to make flour, two other ingredients appear. When pressed, the pulp releases a white juice. If left for a while, all of the starch in it sinks to the bottom. Particularly in the Amazon, the remaining juice is put aside to ferment naturally; in other parts of Brazil, it is thrown away. The starch is still known as tapioca, the name given it by the Tupis, members of the largest indigenous group that originally inhabited Brazil. I say this to highlight the fact that this word (and the technique that it implies), which has become well known all over the world, is Brazilian, part of the culture of the peoples who lived here before colonization. As a Brazilian, I was surprised when I went to Europe, Asia and the United States and discovered that people knew tapioca. And, then they told me that the starchy pellets had Asian roots!

How to explain this? The great maritime explorations of the Age of Discovery led, without doubt, to the largest and most important gastronomic movement in human history. The discovery and exploitation of new continents and the natural exchange of ingredients to which these ventures gave rise provoked revolutions in the eating ways and habits of many peoples. Spices came from Asia. The Americas exported tomatoes, potatoes, corn (maize) and also tapioca. For some reason, the Chinese used it more. And the use of an ingredient assists its survival. Unfortunately, at that time, the inhabitants of Brazil did not know how to claim paternity and authorship of tapioca. But I don't see this is as a problem. The good news is that someone used and therefore helped to preserve tapioca. I like this story because it fits well with what I try to do as a matter of course in my restaurant. I try to develop the possibilities for using ingredients. With creativity, bien sûr.

Oyster pane with tapioca marinée

SERVES 4

	Ingredients	Preparation
Sago	• 100 g sago • 50 ml lime juice • salt	• Place the sago in a large pan with 1 litre of water and cook over medium heat until tender. The sago pearls should still be white in the centre and not completely transparent. • Drain the sago and submerge in plety of ice water to stop the cooking process. • Drain again, combine with the lime juice, season with salt and set aside.
Oysters	• 4 medium oysters • 2 eggs • 100 g brioche flour • olive oil, for frying • 4 drops tabasco sauce • salt and pepper	• Open the oysters, being careful to retain the water inside them. • Add the oyster water to the sago and set aside. • Beat the eggs in a shallow bowl and season with salt and pepper. • Take an oyster and dip in the beaten egg, then roll it in the brioche flour. Repeat with the remaining oysters. • Heat some olive oil in a frying pan or skillet and pan-fry the oysters until golden. • Lay the oysters on absorbent kitchen paper to remove any unwanted grease. • Place a drop of tabasco sauce on each of the oysters.
Soy sauce emulsion	• 50 ml olive oil • 5 ml soy sauce	• Mix the oil and soy sauce until well combined. Set aside.

Finish and presentation

• **2 tablespoons salmon roe**
• **4 chives, finely chopped**

• Place a spoonful of soy sauce emulsion on a small plate.
• Top with a fried oyster and a spoonful of sago.
• Add salmon roe to taste and a scattering of chopped chives.

Tucupi

The final manioc subproduct comes from the processing of the juice produced when grated manioc is pressed, and is made in the Amazon region. This juice is rich in a substance called cyanidric acid, which is extremely harmful to human health. One indication of manioc's toxicity, as our ancestors knew, is its naturally yellow colouration. But once it has been fermented and cooked for a day with local herbs, the poisonous cyanidric acid is vaporized and tucupi is born. Fermentation, it is worth noting, is a fundamental element of Amazonian culture. The hot, humid climate of this vast region means that the process occurs spontaneously there. The indigenous tribespeople of the region know that from inherited wisdom and their own experiments, and use it to conserve ingredients as well as to generate flavour and produce alcohol. Indeed, some wines, spirits and beers originate in that region and often these liquids have medicinal properties.

One of the results of this fermentation process is tucupi. It is a yellow, acidic, stable liquid. One of the most common ways of conserving foods in the Amazon is cooking animal protein in tucupi. The technique has similarities to escabeche and to pickling in vinegar. But tucupi has a unique and potent flavour. In some regions of the Amazon it is the most representative element of local culture.

Onion with tucupi

SERVES 4

	Ingredients	Preparation
Onion	• **300 g onion** • **600 g beetroot** • **5 soup spoons butter**	• Pre-heat the oven to 180°C/350°F. • Peel the onion and cut into 3-cm slices. Set aside. • Peel the beetroot, place in a blender and process to a juice. Set aside. • Place a little butter in the bottom of a small ovenproof dish. Add the onions and ¾ of the beet juice. • Cover with aluminium foil, place in the oven and bake for 25 minutes. • At the end of this time, add the remaining beet juice and bake for 5 minutes more. • Remove from the oven and set aside.
Tucupi	• **2 ml xanthan** • **350 ml tucupi** • **25 g coriander (cilantro)** • **30 g aromatic pepper** • **½ spicy aromatic pepper** • **salt**	• In a small bowl mix the xanthan with 20 ml of water to a thick, smooth cream. • Place the tucupi, coriander (cilantro) and peppers in a small pan. Heat to simmering point and simmer over low heat, stirring from time to time, for about 20 minutes. Do not allow to boil. • Remove from the heat and season with salt. Strain, then add the xanthan and mix to a creamy consistency. Set aside.

Finish and Presentation

• **1 piece bottarga**

• Using a fine grater, grind the bottarga to a powder and set aside.
• Return the onion to the oven for a few seconds to warm.
• Place a spoonful of the tucupi sauce on a dish and arrange a serving of the onion on top.
• Finish with a sprinkling of the bottarga powder alongside the sauce.

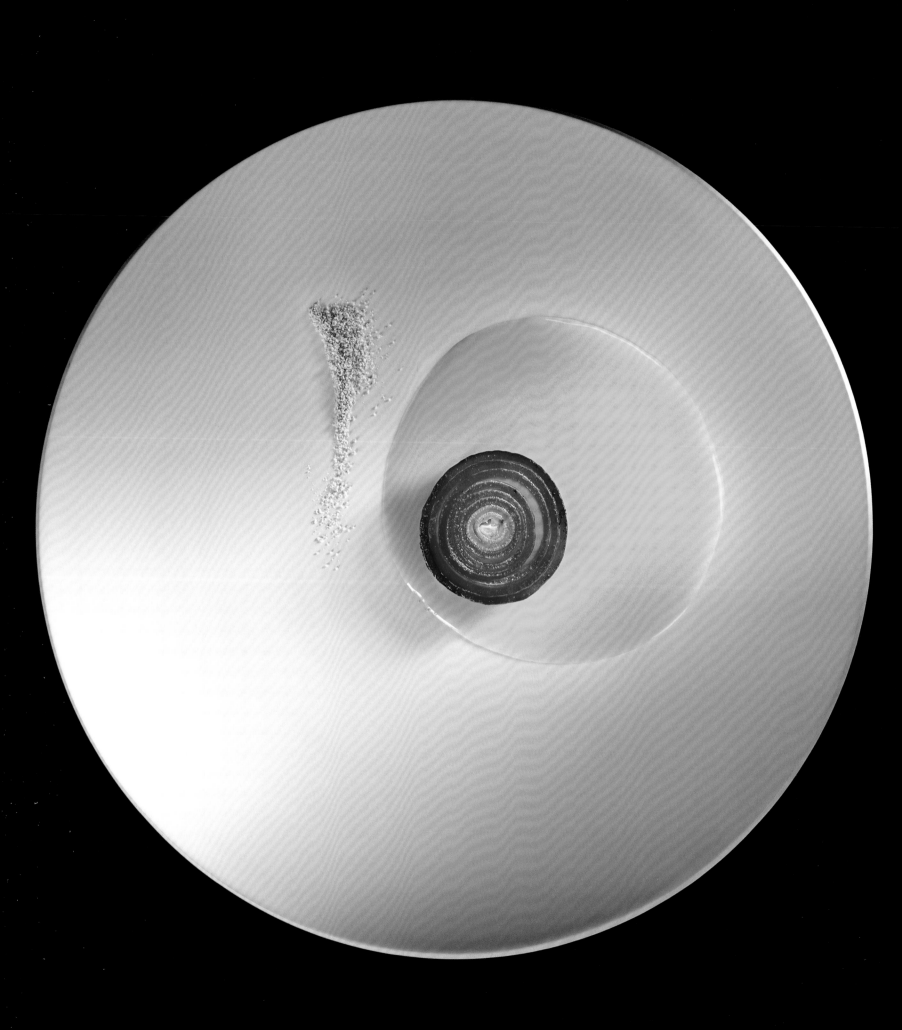

Shrimp with tucupi

SERVES 4

	Ingredients	**Preparation**	**Finish and presentation**
Shrimp and jambu	• **500 g dried shrimp** • **300 g jambu leaves**	• Soak the shrimp for 4 hours in cold water, then drain. • Cook the shrimp in a pan of boiling water for 3 minutes. Remove from water and set aside. • Use the shrimp cooking water to blanche the jambu leaves for 2 minutes. • Remove the jambu from the pan and immediately submerge in ice water. Set aside.	• **black salt** • **chives** • Place a ladleful of the cassava into a bowl. • Add a ladleful of the tucupi broth. • Top with 4 shrimps and a sprig of jambu and serve.
Cassava	• **500g cassava starch**	• Dissolve the cassava starch in 300 ml water. Set aside. • Heat 400 ml water in a medium pan until boiling. Add the starch mixture and cook for 5 minutes, stirring constantly, until translucent and thick.	
Tucupi broth	• **2 litres tucupi** • **10 g basil, leaves torn** • **10 g sawtooth coriander, leaves torn** • **2 cloves garlic** • **2 spicy aromatic peppers, chopped**	• Place the tucupi, basil, coriander, garlic and peppers in a large saucepan and heat to a gentle simmer. Cook for 5 minutes, set aside and keep warm.	

The vegetarian tasting menu

When looking at the vast range of Brazilian ingredients, we soon realize that the most incredible tastes come from the earth. Vegetarianism is thus a natural consequence of the appreciation of Brazilian ingredients that I have been promoting at D.O.M. I am not a part of any movement preaching the consumption – or the non-consumption – of meat. I think a chef must work with his ingredients – he cannot favour one category over another. But when we decided to give prominence to the character, texture and personality of the sublime ingredients present in Brazil it was vegetables that appeared in the greatest number. Dishes with vegetables started gaining more and more space in our tasting menu until, without much effort, a totally vegetarian tasting menu emerged.

D.O.M.'s vegetarian menu is gastronomic. In other words, we use classical reasoning and technique to prepare the dishes. That is why it has none of the frugal overtones generally associated with vegetarian recipes. For instance, we use classic, strong sauces to accompany spaghetti made of palm hearts. And classic cuisine contains many more dishes without animal protein than we could have imagined. This is one of the surprises of the menu.

To accompany these dishes, we have also developed a series of waters flavoured with fruit, spices or herbs. The flavour of each water comes from an ingredient in the dish itself.

We also like to use raw and toasted ingredients. Behind D.O.M.'s philosophy lies a constant search for balance between the modern and the primitive. After all, man goes from nature to culture when he masters fire and starts toasting food. Moreover, preparing raw and toasted foods demands a lot from the chef. Ability and a mastery of technique are needed in order to toast well and to introduce a raw element in to a recipe.

The preparation of the recipes on the vegetarian menu is simple, but it is crucial that their execution be precise in order to surprise the customer and turn that dinner into a unique, memorable experience.

Fruits and nuts

Banana

Among other well-known fruits found in Brazil are the bananas and their relatives the plantains. Plantains, which are invariably cooked before being eaten – toasted (broiled) on a hot iron skillet, fried or roasted – have inimitable flavour and texture. They are most commonly served with fish but are also found at the Brazilian breakfast table.

What we call *banana-ouro*, or golden banana is a mini-banana, 5–8 centimetres long. It is sold in large bunches at the sides of the road leading to São Paulo's coast. The best I can do to describe it is to say that the best perfumes come in the smallest vials, such are the potency of flavour and aroma of this mini-fruit in its small natural package. It is the main component of one of the signature dishes at D.O.M., the Lime and banana ravioli found on page 224 of this book.

Lime and banana ravioli

SERVES 4

	Ingredients	**Preparation**

Priprioca caramel
- 160 g sugar
- 10 ml priprioca essence (see page 186)

- In a medium sized heavy-gauge pan, make a caramel with the sugar reaching a temperature of 142°C /287°F.
- Remove from the heat and carefully add 40 ml of water and the priprioca essence. Set aside.

Crème pâtissière
- 20 g pasteurized egg yolks
- 20 g caster (superfine) sugar
- 4 g plain (all-purpose) flour
- 100 ml milk

- Place the egg yolks, sugar and flour in a bowl and whisk thoroughly.
- Pour the milk into a small pan and bring to the boil.
- Add the milk little by little to the egg mixture while stirring it continuously, to temper the eggs.
- Strain the mixture through a sieve (strainer) into a clean pan and cook it over low heat, stirring constantly, for about 5 minutes.
- Remove from the heat and transfer to a bowl. Cover the bowl with clingfilm (plastic wrap), place in an ice bain-marie to cool.

Lemon and banana ravioli
- 1 baby banana
- 10 g leaf gelatine
- 93 g caster sugar
- 93 ml water
- 50 ml lemon juice
- 1 g agar-agar

- Cut the banana into thin slices.
- Rehydrate the leaf gelatine by placing it in some cold water for a few minutes.
- Place the sugar, water, lemon juice and agar-agar in a pan and warm through stirring constantly over low heat for 5 minutes.
- Remove the pan from the heat and stir in the hydrated gelatine.
- Pour the mixture onto a tray, to a thickness of approximately 2 mm.
- When set, cut into rounds with a circular 5-cm cutter.

Sugar syrup
- 250 g caster sugar
- 250 ml water

- Place the sugar and water in a pan and heat through to dissolve, then bring to the boil and remove immediately from the heat.

Lime zest confit
- zest of ½ lime
- sugar syrup

- Have ready a bowl of water with plenty of ice.
- Bring a pan of water to the boil and blanch the strips of lime zest briefly before plunging them into the ice water to cool.
- Repeat this procedure 3 times then drain the zests.
- Heat the sugar syrup and add the blanched zests.

Finish and Presentation

- To assemble the raviolis, place a round of gelatine on the plate and drop a little crème pâtissière in the centre.
- Position 3 thin banana slices over the gelatine round and finish with another layer of gelatine.
- Using a pastry bag, finish the raviolis with a drop of crème pâtissière on top and decorate with 2 pieces of lime zest.
- Place 3 raviolis in the centre of the plate.
- Finish with a drizzle of the priprioca caramel.

Crunchy banana cappelletti

SERVES 4

	Ingredients	Preparation	Finish and presentation
Tangerine sorbet	• 240 ml tangerine pulp concentrate • 2 egg whites	• Place all the ingredients with 450 ml water in a bowl and mix thoroughly. Transfer to a Pacojet beaker. • Place in the freezer until frozen. Blend in the Pacojet before serving.	• Arrange a serving of warm cappelletti on a plate. • Drizzle some of the passion fruit syrup over the top of the cappelletti, with a little more on the plate. • Place a quenelle of the tangerine sorbet to one side of the cappelletti.
Banana filling	• 9 bananas • 75 g caster (superfine) sugar • 1 pinch cinnamon powder	• Finely chop the bananas and mix in a large bowl with the sugar and a pinch of cinnamon powder. • Place a large stainless steel frying pan or skillet over low heat. • Add the banana mixture and cook over low heat, stirring often, for about 1 hour or until the banana pieces no longer adhere to the pan and are crunchy. • Transfer from the pan to a baking sheet, allow to cool and set aside in the refrigerator.	
Passion fruit syrup	• 500 g passion fruit pulp • 50 g caster sugar • 50 ml passion fruit juice concentrate	• Place all the ingredients in a medium pan with 50 ml water and cook over low heat, stirring until the sugar is dissolved. • Continue cooking over low heat, stirring occasionally, until it has reduced to a thick syrup. Set aside.	
Banana cappelletti	• 150 g spring roll wrappers • banana filling (above) • 2 egg whites • clarified butter, for greasing	• Pre-heat the oven to 180°C/350°F and put some serving plates to warm. • Cut the spring roll wrappers into 7.5-cm x 7.5-cm squares. • Place a spoonful of the filling in the centre of the dough. • Dampen the edges of the dough with the egg white, then place another square on top and press the edges together, as for cappelletti. • Grease a baking sheet with the clarified butter and spread the cappelletti on it. • Bake for 5 minutes or until the cappelletti are golden brown.	

Cupuaçu

Of all the strange, characterful fruit in Brazil, the most interesting one may be *cupuaçu*, an ancestor of cocoa. Exotic, full of character and somewhat strange, it is a hard, thick-skinned fruit with a flavour and aroma reminiscent of chemicals such as ether, but a sweetness and texture that bring it back to the edible universe.

Its pulp, which is rich in pectin, is often used to prepare jams and conserves. Its pods are fermented and toasted to produce a drink that is halfway between coffee and chocolate.

Oyster with cupuaçu

SERVES 4

	Ingredients	Preparation	Finish and presentation
Cupuaçu sorbet	• 150 g caster (superfine) sugar • 2 teaspoons liquid glucose • 100 g cupuaçu pulp (see page 228) • juice of 1 lime	• Place the sugar and glucose in a pan with 150 ml water and stir over low heat to dissolve. • Heat to 110°C/230°F and maintain at this temperature until a syrup is formed. • Incorporate the cupuaçu pulp and set aside to cool. • Stir in the lime juice and transfer to a Pacojet beaker. • Freeze, ready to process in the Pacojet just before serving.	• 10 ml bourbon • black salt • 4 clover sprouts • Place one oyster in its shell on a plate. • Pour 2.5 ml whiskey over the oyster. • Place a small quenelle of the sorbet next to the oyster and decorate with a mango crispy. • Finish with a few grains of black salt and a clover sprout.
Mango crispies	• ½ vanilla pod • 150 g fresh mango • 44 g glucose	• Preheat the oven to 130°C/265°F and place a Silpat on a baking sheet. • Slit the vanilla pod lengthwise and scrape out the seeds. • Blend the seeds with the mango in a blender and pass the mixture through a sieve (strainer) into a clean bowl. • Place the glucose in a pan and melt over low heat, then incorporate into the mango and vanilla mixture. • Pour this mixture onto the Silpat in a very thin layer and bake for 35–40 minutes, or until crunchy. • Set aside in a cool, dry place.	
Oysters	• 4 medium oysters	• Shuck the oysters and drain the liquor. • Return the oysters to their shells.	

Bacuri and pequi

Among the huge variety of Amazonian fruit *bacuri* is one of my favourites. I believe that its sweetness, acidity, floral notes and dry aroma make this fruit of simple appearance superior to the Far Eastern mangosteen and rambutan.

It grows only in the north of Piauí, Maranhão and Pará between February and May so is not available for much of the year. It has a peculiar shape, thick skin and a central seed surrounded by white pulp.

Another distictive Brazilian fruit is *pequi* (image opposite). Its strong flavour has a hint of cheese that it is often disliked by non Brazilians. When used sparingly, it adds an intriguing and uplifting flavour note to heavier dishes, such as Cupim with potato purée and pequi (see page 46).

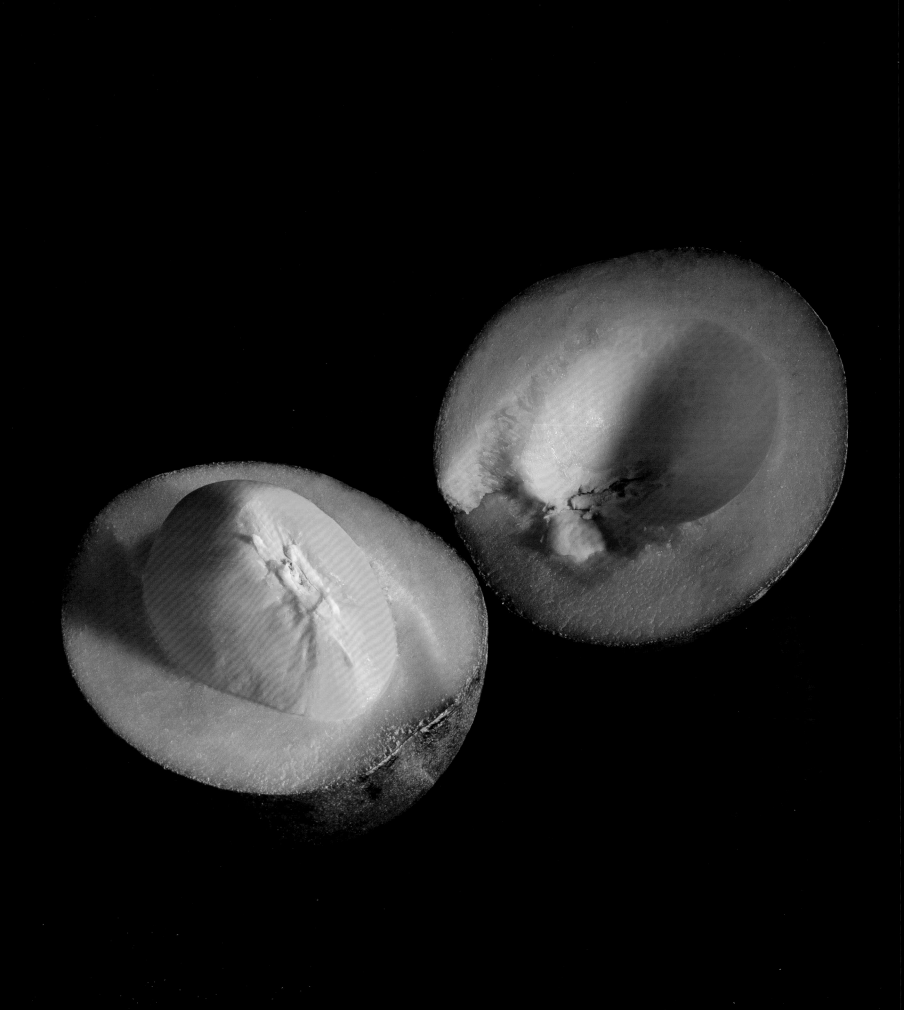

Sea urchin with bacuri

SERVES 4

Ingredients	Preparation	Finish and Presentation
Kombu and katsuobushi broth		
• **15 cm kombu seaweed** • **20 g katsuobushi**	• Place the kombu in a medium pan with 500 ml water. • Heat to 80°C/175°F. • Remove the kombu from the pan and set aside. • Place the katsuobushi in the same water, bring to the boil and boil for 5 minutes then remove from the heat. • Remove the katsuobushi and set aside. Reserve the broth.	• **1 small yam, peeled and washed** • **4 drops lemon juice** • **20 g red bell pepper** • **40 g bacuri pulp** • **wakame (reserved from second step)** • **peel of 1 lemon** • **50 g mint leaves**
Seaweed broth		
• **Kombu and katsuoboshi broth (above)** • **20 ml soy sauce** • **5 slices ginger** • **30 g aromatic pepper** • **½ hot chilli pepper** • **100 g bacuri pulp** • **5 g dried wakame**	• In a medium pan, heat the broth, soy sauce, ginger, both peppers and the bacuri pulp. • When the liquid reaches a temperature of 70°C/160°F, add the wakame. • Continue to cook, without boiling, over low heat for about 25 minutes to allow the ingredients to release their flavours. • Strain through a cloth or very fine chinois, reserving the seaweed broth and setting aside the wakame for the finish and presentation • When cold, cover and place in the refrigerator.	• Use a knife or a comb mandoline with a narrow setting to cut the yam into square sticks 2 cm long. Place in a bowl of cold water with 4 drops of lemon juice. • Chop the red bell pepper to a brunoise of 2 mm x 2 mm and set aside. • Lay 10 g of bacuri pulp in the base of a glass bowl.
Sea urchin		
• **4 sea urchins**	• Remove the top of the sea urchins and drain off any water from inside. • Carefully remove the orange roe with a spoon, rinse in cold water and set aside.	• Place a small portion of the reserved wakame seaweed over the bacuri pulp, then place a sea urchin gently beside it. • Using the tip of a small spoon carefully place a little chopped red pepper brunoise on top of the sea urchin. • Drain the yam sticks from the acidulated water and arrange about 15 sticks in the bowl. • Cut the mint into a fine chiffonade and scatter a little over the sea urchin. • Gently pour over enough of the broth to cover the sea urchin. • Finally, twist the lemon peel over the dish to flavour it.

Green papaya, yogurt and bacuri

SERVES 4

	Ingredients	Preparation	Finish and Presentation
Green papaya	• **1 small green papaya** • **100 g quicklime** • **1 kg caster (superfine) sugar** • **30 g coriander seeds**	• Peel the green papaya and use a mandoline to cut it in 12-cm x 2-cm strips. • Being very careful that it does not make contact with your skin, dissolve the quicklime in 1 litre of water, place the papaya in the mixture and let it sit for 10 minutes. • Carefully remove the papaya from the quicklime solution and wash thoroughly in running water. • In a large pan, place 1 litre of water, the sugar and the coriander seeds. Add the washed papaya and simmer on low heat for 3 hours. • Cool, cover and set aside in the refrigerator.	• **powdered yogurt** • **edible white flowers, to garnish** • Place curls of the papaya strips on the plate and scatter the yogurt powder over them. • Decorate the dish with the flowers and finish with a light covering of the bacuri snow.
Bacuri snow	• **80 g bacuri**	• Blend the bacuri and 120 ml water in the Thermomix to obtain a homogeneous mixture. Place this mixture into a Pacojet beaker and freeze to -17°C/1.4°F. • Blend in the Pacojet until it is the consistency of snow.	

Pitanga

Pitanga is familiar to all Brazilians, but nobody can buy it because it is not grown commercially, being limited to back yards and seashores. In the last few years, the city of São Paulo has been widely reforested with pitanga trees. It is common to find several trees linked together. They attract a lot of birds, as well as eager passers by, keen to share the spoils.

It is hard to describe the flavour of such a distinctly Brazilian fruit. It is at once sweet, tart and pungent with an enduring flavour. Its delicate shape is reminiscent of a tiny pumpkin, but its intense red-orange colour goes some way to indicate the shock of flavour that it contains.

Lamb with yam purée and pitanga

SERVES 4

	Ingredients	**Preparation**	**Finish and Presentation**

Lamb shanks

Ingredients:
- 4 lamb shanks
- 1 bay leaf
- 1 rosemary sprig
- 1 thyme sprig
- rapeseed (canola) oil
- 2 carrots
- 2 onions
- 3 tomatoes
- 1 celery stick
- 2 leeks
- 5 cloves garlic
- 200 ml white wine
- salt and pepper

Preparation:
- Trim the excess fat and nerves from the shanks and season them with salt and pepper.
- Roughly chop the herbs and place in a bowl with the shanks, rubbing them into the surface of the meat then, cover and leave in the refrigerator to infuse for 24 hours.
- After this time, gently scrape the herbs from the meat and set aside.
- Next heat a frying pan or skillet, add a dash of oil and seal the shanks.
- Cut the vegetables into medium-sized cubes.
- Heat a large pan and add a little oil then fry the vegetables.
- Add the shanks, the wine and the reserved herbs from the marinade and cover all with water.
- Bring to simmering point and allow to simmer over low heat for 3 hours or until the shanks are very tender.

Yam purée

Ingredients:
- 1 kg yam
- 300 ml milk
- 80 g unsalted butter
- 200 ml double (heavy) cream
- salt and pepper

Preparation:
- Bring a large pan of salted water to the boil (enough to cover the yams) and cook them whole in their skins until soft.
- Drain and peel the yams.
- Chop the flesh finely and place in the Thermomix with the milk. Beat well.
- In a large pan, heat the butter and the cream, then add the yam mixture.
- Cook over low heat for about 20 minutes, stirring occasionally. Season to taste.

Finish and Presentation
- olive oil, for frying
- 100 g button mushrooms, cut in half
- 2 cloves garlic, finely chopped
- 200 ml lamb jus
- 50 ml pitanga juice (see page 238)
- 4 peppermint leaves, fried
- 4 pitanga fruits

- Heat a frying pan or skillet and add a dash of olive oil, then brown the mushrooms.
- Add the chopped garlic, season with salt and set aside.
- Heat the lamb jus in a pan over low heat and, once simmering, add the pitanga juice.
- Preheat the oven to 200°C/400°F. Debone the lamb and trim the edges. Place in a roasting pan and brush with the jus to glaze.
- Place in the preheated oven for about 5 minutes, then remove from the oven and brush with the glaze again.
- Heat the yam purée in the Thermomix at 80°C /175°F.
- Spread a dash of the yam purée on a plate, then place a serving of the lamb in the centre of the plate.
- Decorate with a few mushroom halves, a fried peppermint leaf and a pitanga fruit.

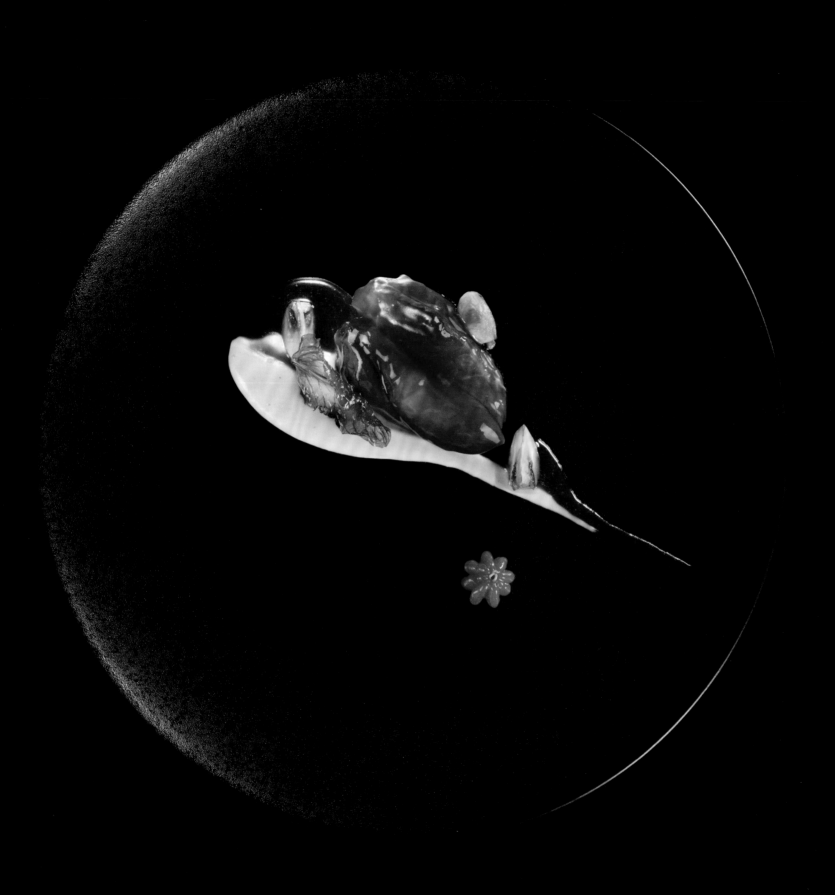

Citrus fruit

In this book I have tried to focus on native Brazilian ingredients in a desire to show the roots of Brazil. However, many fruit that the world imagines to be Brazilian have actually been introduced. Mangoes, starfruit and jackfruit are not native. Others, such as coconuts and bananas, have always been present in Brazil but do not have a defined botanical origin. Brazil is a colonized country. It has received immigrants from all corners of the world, which has turned it into a dense, complex and curious cultural mosaic. If one thinks like this, the children of Arabs, Japanese, French and Dutchmen who were born in Brazil are Brazilian. Following this argument, it is not unreasonable to regard the many fruit that were introduced here as being Brazilian too.

 I want to talk about a fruit that is not Brazilian, but is used so frequently in Brazil and is so little known in the rest of the world, that, even though it is not native, deserves to be treated as if it were. This citrus fruit is not acidic, and has a potent aroma; its juice, a few minutes after being extracted, develops an elegant bitterness. It is sweet lime. Here we call it *lima-da-pérsia*, or Persian lime. I think a citrus fruit that is not acidic can be compared to a sugar that is not sweet: it seems strange, but it is fascinating. This flavour of sweet lime adds a sense of exuberance to a dish. Generally speaking, in every recipe in which I use it, I exaggerate. And it always works.

Another fascinating citrus fruit is the rangpur. In Brazil, we call it *limão cravo*, *limão-rosa* or *limão-vinagre* – clove lime, pink lime or vinegar lime. The explanation for those names is very simple. Clove lime comes from its acidity which feels like a spike, or a clove, on the tongue. It is also a lime with an intense colour, and, in this part of the world, it has become pink. Vinegar lime refers to its high juice content.

This ingredient is commonly found and widely used in the Brazilian countryside, but it is rarely encountered in stores because of its looks. When the fruit is ripe, oxidation marks on the surface make it ugly. So it is shunned by supermarkets even though it is abundant in the back yards and home cooking of Brazil.

Baby pork ribs with Persian lime and cornmeal porridge

SERVES 4

	Ingredients	Preparation	Finish and presentation
Baby pork ribs	• 800 g pork ribs, cut into 2-rib portions • 2 sprigs parsley, roughly chopped • 1 sprig peppermint, roughly chopped • 2 onions, finely chopped • 3 cloves garlic, finely chopped • 2 carrots, finely chopped • 1 spicy aromatic pepper, finely chopped • canola (rapeseed) oil • 6 tomatoes, finely chopped • 1 bay leaf • 300 ml white wine • 50 ml white wine vinegar • salt and pepper	• In a large dish season the ribs with salt and pepper and add the herbs, onions, garlic, carrots and chilli. • Cover, transfer to the refrigerator and leave to marinate for 24 hours. • Heat a dash of rapeseed (canola) oil in a large pan, remove the meat from the marinade and pan-fry until golden on both sides. • Add the vegetables from the marinade along with the tomatoes and bay leaf and sauté for ten minutes. • Add the wine and continue to cook until evaporated. • Add the herbs from the marinade to the pan and add water until the meat is just covered. Simmer for 4 hours or until the meat is tender. Remove the meat and set aside. • Strain the liquid and return to the pan over low heat until reduced by half. Set aside.	• 1 Persian lime, sliced • 1 onion, finely sliced • olive oil, for frying • 4 pearl onions, peeled and cut in half • zest from 1 Persian lime • 4 edible sprouts • Preheat the oven to 200°C/400°F. • Brush the ribs with the tamarind purée and place in the oven for 30 seconds. Remove from the oven and repeat this process twice more. • Spread the lime slices on a baking sheet and place under a preheated grill (broiler), turning halfway through, until lightly browned on both sides. • Place the sliced onion in a frying pan or skillet with a dash of oil and slowly caramelize over low heat until soft, sweet and golden. • Pre-heat a dry frying pan or skillet and toast the pearl onion halves. • When nicely coloured remove the onions from the pan, separate the petals and set aside. • Heat the reserved pork cooking sauce over low heat without letting it boil. Add the lime zest. • Spoon a serving of the sauce into a wide, shallow bowl. • Place a spoonful of cornmeal (maize) porridge in the centre of the bowl and top with a portion of pork ribs. • Place a slice of the grilled (broiled) lime beside the porridge. • Place a dot of tamarind purée inside each of the pearl onion petals and place them around the dish. • Garnish with an edible sprout.
Tamarind purée	• 500 g tamarind pulp • 80 g caster (superfine) sugar	• Place the tamarind pulp and sugar in a pan over low heat and cook, stirring occasionally, until the mixture has turned syrupy. • Remove from the heat, allow to cool and transfer to the refrigerator until needed.	
Cornmeal porridge	• 200 g savoury cornmeal (maize) porridge • 1 onion, finely chopped • 80 g unsalted butter, plus extra to taste • salt	• Place the porridge in a pan with 1 litre of water and cook over low heat for 40 minutes. Set aside. • Sauté the onion with the butter in a pan over low heat and add the cooked savoury maize porridge. Cook for 5 minutes and add a small amount of butter until the mixture reaches a creamy consistency. Season with salt and reserve.	

Jabuticaba

The *jabuticaba* tree is quite common in Brazilian gardens and back yards, especially in São Paulo. A member of the Myrtaceae family, and native to the rainforests, the *jabuticaba* takes around ten years to show fruit. After that, if it gets enough water, it will produce fruit twice a year.

The city of São Paulo has a huge population, over 11 million, which includes the world's largest Japanese community outside Japan. I grew up in São Paulo surrounded by both *jabuticaba* fruit and wasabi, a well-known Japanese ingredient. I put the two together and created an ice cream from them (see page 248).

The *jabuticaba* fruit grows on both the branches and the trunk of the tree. When mature it has a thick, dark red skin, almost black, and one big seed cocooned in an extremely sweet white body.
After boiling, the *jabuticaba* skin becomes a beautiful intense rose colour, almost lilac. I made my ice cream from the boiled fruit and then added the wasabi. This is a beautiful, delicious recipe that sums up São Paulo absolutely.

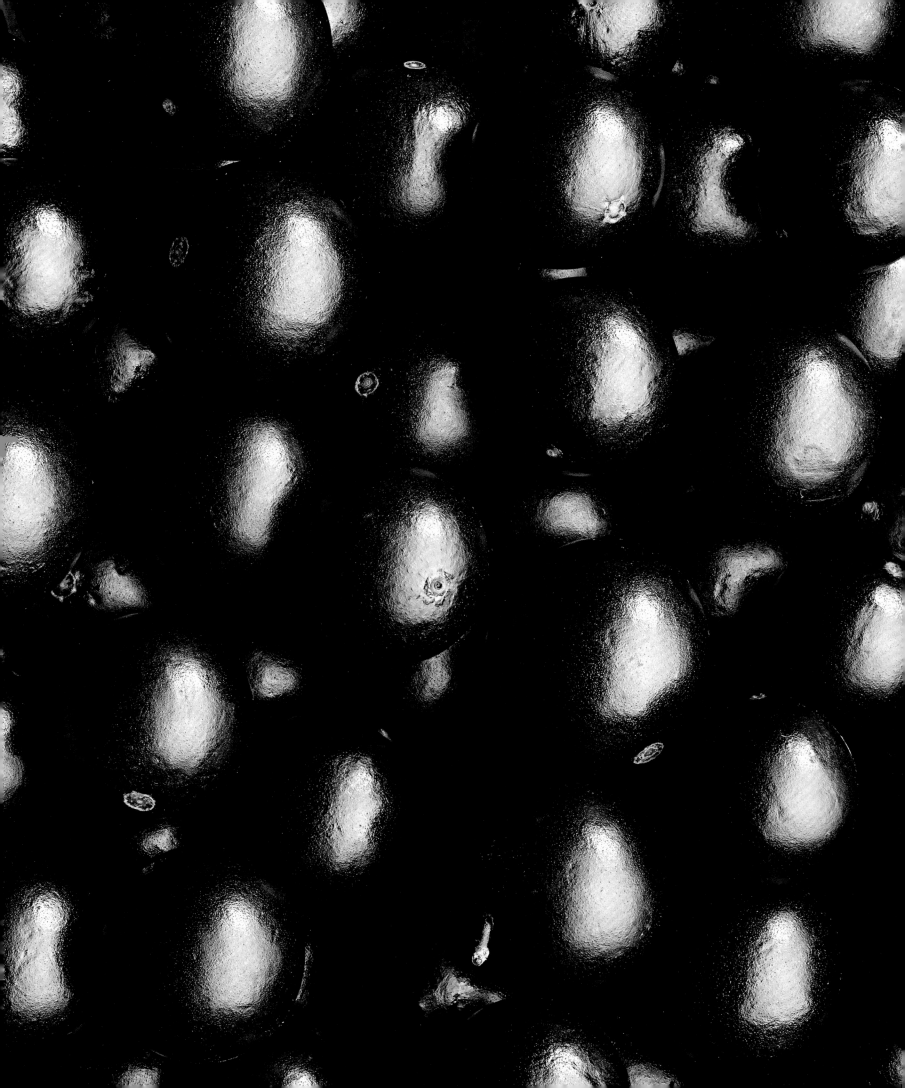

Jabuticaba with wasabi sorbet

SERVES 4

	Ingredients	Preparation	Finish and Presentation
Jabuticaba syrup	• **1 kg jabuticaba fruits** • **500 g caster (superfine) sugar**	• Tear the jabuticaba fruits roughly and place them in a saucepan. • Add 3 litres of water and the sugar and cook over low heat, without boiling, until reduced to 1 litre. • Strain the syrup through a fine sieve (strainer) into a clean bowl and reserve	• Place a serving of the sorbet in a dish and serve.
Sorbet	• **375 g jabuticaba syrup (above)** • **140 g caster sugar** • **20 ml raspberry vinegar** • **20 ml lemon juice** • **15 g wasabi** • **80 g egg white**	• Using a mixer beat all the ingredients with 100 ml water until frothy. • Place the mixture in the ice cream machine and process according to the instructions.	

Other Brazilian fruits

The range of home-grown fruit available in Brazilian markets gets wider every day. There are so many that I couldn't possibly include them all in this book, but they are part of cultural register and one of the reasons that Brazilian cuisine is so unique.

When I opened D.O.M. in 1999 I used *cambuci* in some recipes. It is a fruit with a strong, tart, fragrant taste, which I remember from my childhood. When customers asked me if it came from the Amazon, I told them that it was in fact a wild fruit from our own region, from the rainforest on the Atlantic seaboard.

Another fruit that must be mentioned is *jambul* (image opposite) which comes from some of the most incredible trees in Brazil. When its flowers open, their violet, scarlet shade contrasts strongly with that of the large green leaves. As the flowers start to fall they form thick carpets on the ground. A few days later, the fruit appears. With its unique purple shade, this fruit, which has a delicate, crunchy and watery texture, has no great taste or acidity; but its floral aroma, similar to roses, is scary. It is perhaps the sexiest of Brazilian fruit. It has been mentioned countless times in our literature, which compares its colour and aroma to the lips and perfume of Brazil's beautiful women.

Until the 1990s, the Brazilian government operated an anti-import policy. Once the markets were opened, people were awestruck and everyone got drunk on imported ingredients. In the ice-cream business, for instance, the average Brazilian soon got acquainted with pistachio, hazelnut and new berries. These flavours were not entirely unknown to us, but they were not present in our daily lives.

Now, with some pride, I am noticing a different movement. A good number of ice-cream manufacturers have started to dedicate a large part of their production to Brazilian fruit. Nor does the success of our fruit stop there: from time to time I receive emails and photos showing our fruit in Japan, the United States and European countries. And I am more and more convinced that, if there exists today a new frontier of flavours and taste sensations, it goes through Brazil.

Brazilian vanilla

As a professional chef, I have always liked vanilla. I liked it even more after I learned that it was derived from an orchid. A curious fact: all reddish orchids trace their origin to South America.

We have a huge variety of orchids in Brazil. The most fascinating of them grows in the Cerrado, an arid region in the middle of the country. In this environment most plants find it hard to survive, but the ones that do grow there contain a large amount of essential oils. From the gastronomic point of view, the region is exciting. It is there that an orchid that produces a giant vanilla bean grows, as big as a banana. This bean, when dry, develops an inimitable aroma with clear notes of pipe tobacco. Its taste possibilities intrigue me, but I am especially taken by the potential for social development that this plant offers to the region's inhabitants. In the wild, the orchid has a natural enemy in monkeys. So local women started growing plants in pots and then set up a cooperative to produce high-quality vanilla. The project is still small, but it shows the power that an ingredient can have to galvanize a whole community.

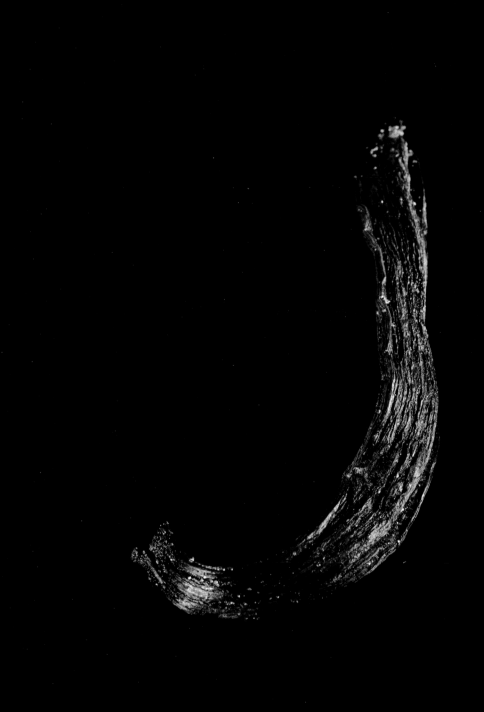

Cornmeal porridge with cheese, sugar cane syrup and vanilla oil

SERVES 4

	Ingredients	Preparation	Finish and presentation
Brazilian vanilla oil	• 1 Brazilian vanilla pod (see page 252) • 250 ml rapeseed (canola) oil	• Slice the vanilla bean in half and place in a pan with the rapeseed (canola) oil. • Heat to 60°C/140°F and then set aside to cool. • Store, covered, at room temperature for at least 5 days before using.	• 60 ml sugar cane syrup • Spoon a portion of the cornmeal (maize) porridge into a wide, shallow bowl. • Using a cook's blowtorch, gently brown the top of the porridge. • Place a cheese crisp next to the porridge. • Finish with a tablespoon of sugar cane syrup and a drizzle of Brazilian vanilla oil.
Cornmeal porridge	• 200 g savoury cornmeal (maize) porridge • 1 onion, finely chopped • 80 g unsalted butter, plus extra to taste • 100 g Serra de Canastra cheese (see page 30), grated • salt	• Place the porridge in a pan with 1 litre of water and cook over low heat for 40 minutes. • Sauté the onion with the butter in a pan over low heat and add the cooked savoury maize porridge. Cook for 5 minutes and add a small amount of butter until the mixture reaches a creamy consistency. • Add the cheese, mix well and season with salt to taste. Set aside.	
Cheese crisp	• 100 g Serra de Canastra cheese, grated	• Heat a frying pan or skillet until very hot and add the cheese. • Allow the cheese to form a crispy crust and the base of the pan and then carefully remove and divide into 4 portions.	

Cocoa

Members of the abundant Brazilian cocoa family are found in the Amazon forest and throughout the Atlantic jungle. Cocoa was first cultivated and extracted in the Atlantic jungle but it was attacked by a plague known as witch's broom, which extinguished its production and trade.

Today, there are some efforts to preserve and once again produce these species of cocoa, especially in the southern region of the state of Bahia. An additional benefit of these efforts – besides the fact that it revives a source of very high-quality chocolate – is in the recuperation of the region's native forest as cocoa needs the shadows of native trees to grow. It also provides an alternative livelihood for whole populations, not to mention the revival of the culture surrounding the cultivation of cocoa.

One of the most fascinating of these initiatives takes place on the island of Combu, a 20-minute boat ride from Belém do Pará. Some decades ago, there was an attempt to cultivate cocoa on Combu and, though the plantation did not prosper, the species that was introduced was successful in taking root and has since become native to the island.

A local woman who used to work in Belém do Pará saw a possibility with this cocoa and now produces about 30 kilos per month. It may seem like a small amount, but if you considers that she picks the fruit; extracts, ferments, toasts and grinds the seeds; and packages her product all alone, the amount gains a new meaning.

With an elegant flavour and rustic, earthy notes, the cocoa produced on this island is one of the biggest revelations of my recent trips to the Amazon. From this, I learned a lesson. We must keep our eyes open. It is easy to assume that new and exciting ingredients will come from the depths of the forest but sometimes they can be found near the urban centres, just under our noses.

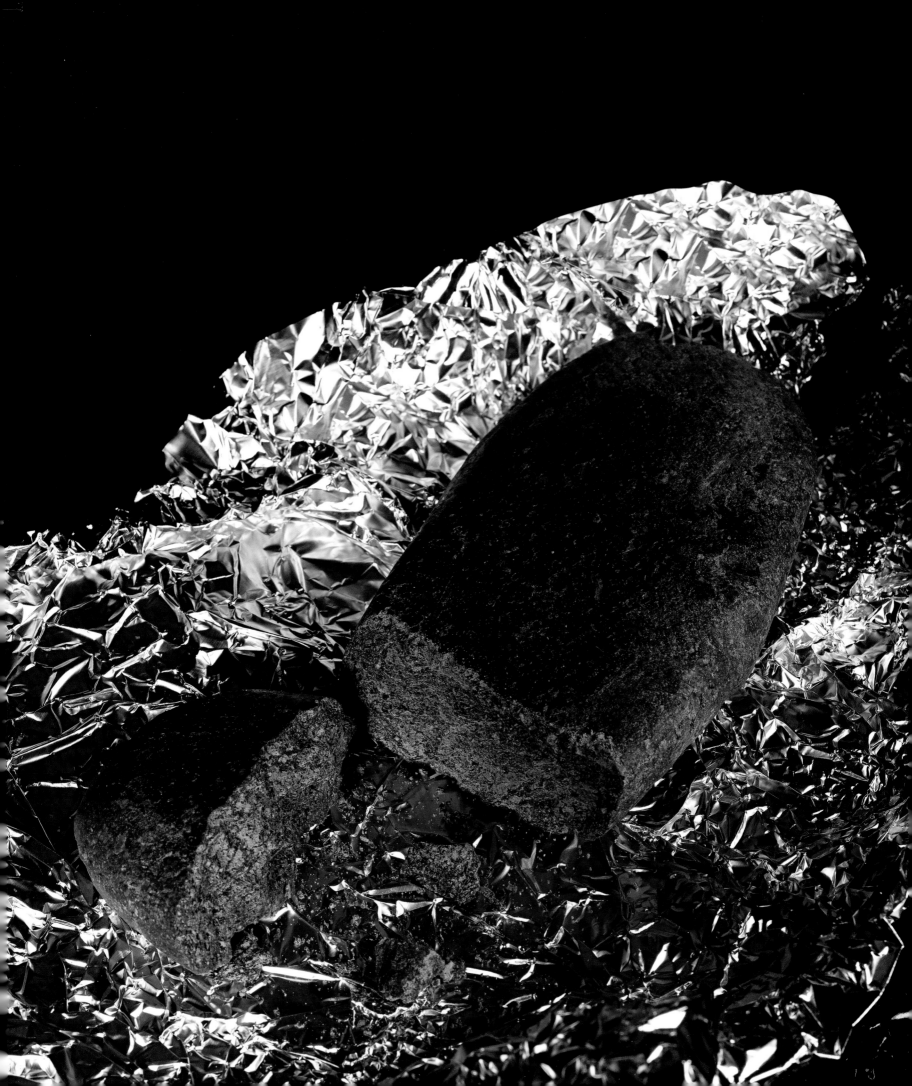

Brazil nut tart with whisky ice cream, chocolate, curry, rocket and salt

SERVES 8

Ingredients

Brazil nut tart
- 50 g caster (superfine) sugar
- 75 g eggs
- 50 g grated brazil nuts
- 17 g breadcrumbs

Chocolate topping
- 12.5 g cocoa powder
- 6 g cornflour (corn starch)
- 125 g 64% cocoa chocolate
- 62.5 g butter
- 2 g soy lecithin
- 117 g caster sugar
- 90 g glucose

Whisky ice cream
- 125 ml double (heavy) cream
- 125 ml milk
- 50 g caster sugar
- 80 g pasteurized egg yolks
- 50 ml whisky

Preparation

- Using a mixer, beat the sugar and eggs together until pale.
- Add the brazil nuts to the mixture and incorporate thoroughly, then stir in the breadcrumbs.
- Pour the mixture into a silicone mould and bake at 170°C/340°F for 12 minutes.
- When cool, remove the tart from the mould and set aside.

- Beat the cocoa powder and cornstarch with 93.5 ml water in the Thermomix and cook on a low setting until it reaches 70°C/160°F.
- Add the chocolate, butter, lecithin and sugar. Mix well and continue to cook on the low setting until it reaches 70°C/160°F again.
- Add the glucose and continue to cook until it reaches 80°C/176°F.
- Sieve (strain) the mixture through a fine chinois into a clean bowl, allow to cool then cover and set aside.

- In a medium pan, mix the cream with the milk and half the sugar and bring it to the boil.
- In a bowl, beat the yolks with the remaining sugar until pale.
- Add the egg mixture to the milk and cook over low heat until it reaches 82°C/180°F.
- Remove from the heat and sieve through a fine chinois into a clean bowl.
- Add the whisky, and when the mixture has cooled, place it in an ice cream machine and process until it reaches a creamy consistency.

Finish and Presentation

- 1 tablespoon curry powder
- Maldon sea salt
- cumari pepper oil
- mini rocket (arugula)

- In a deep dish, make a swirling trace with the chocolate topping.
- Sprinkle the curry powder over the chocolate and bowl of the dish.
- Position a portion of the Brazil nut tart over part of the topping.
- Sprinkle a little Maldon sea salt, a drop of pepper oil and a few leaves of mini rocket over the serving.
- To finish, add a quenelle of whisky ice cream.

Coconut

Botanists find it difficult to pinpoint the origin of coconuts, referring only to our planet's tropical latitudes. It is easy to understand why: coconuts fall from palm trees on the coast, then waves float them to the next beach. It was in this way, presumably, that this gastronomical jewel spread itself around the world. For us Brazilians, inhabitants of a tropical climate, drinking green coconut water on the beach means being in harmony with the sea and with nature. The gastronomic possibilities of the coconut are incredible, for instance, there are countless fascinating, delicious sweets made of coconut in Brazil. The milk is often used to in the preparation of both sweet and savoury dishes. The flesh, while still unripe, has a gelatinous, clam-like texture, and, if cut like squid rings, can confer elegance on Asian salads.

Quindim

Quindim

SERVES 4

Ingredients

- 62 g pasteurized egg yolk
- 70 g caster (superfine)sugar, plus extra for coating the moulds
- 23 g grated fresh coconut
- 7 g butter melted, plus extra for greasing

Preparation

- Grease 4 x 2-cm moulds with butter and coat lightly with sugar.
- Place all the ingredients except the butter in a large bowl and mix well.
- Divide the mixture between the 4 moulds, place them on a baking sheet and set aside to rest for 30 minutes.
- Preheat the oven to 90°C/195°F
- Bake in the preheated oven for 10 minutes.
- Set aside cool before removing from the moulds and serving.

Coconut apple

Here in Brazil we have a special way of using coconuts. When the ripe fruit falls from the tree and the seed finds a good spot to germinate, it sprouts to generate another plant. At the exact moment of germination the coconut water becomes almost solid, with a sponge-like texture and unique flavour. We call it the apple of the coconut, and it does not taste quite like regular coconut water, flesh or milk. With an appearance that few will associate with coconut, and yet a taste that will remind everyone of coconut, it can be used in many ways in the kitchen.

Nature brings us food in unimagined places. A few years ago, just after a riptide, standing by a still agitated, muddy sea, I found some ingredients in the sand. That day I included algae and the coconut sprout, 'the apple', in my cooking.

Unfortunately, these two ingredients were lost among plastic bags, cans and other detritus brought in by the sea. That experience resulted in some new recipes and a reflection: the sea itself is not an endless resource; it is the possibilities for using the things that the sea brings us that are endless. The planet today has 7 billion inhabitants. Pessimists believe that, when population reaches somewhere between 9 and 12 billion, everything will collapse because there will be not enough food for so many people. Refuting this are optimists who say that we already produce enough food for 20 billion people. We can join those optimists if we start improving the way we use ingredients: using 100 per cent of an ingredient should not be restricted to times of hardship. A walk on the beach after a riptide showed me that even a polluted sea is generous and full of potential.

Coconut apple with seaweed, turnip, radish and cumaru vinaigrette

SERVES 4

	Ingredients	**Preparation**	**Finish and Presentation**
Vanilla oil	• 100 ml rapeseed (canola) oil • ½ Brazilian vanilla pod (see page 252), cut lengthways	• Place the vanilla pod in a pan with the rapeseed (canola) oil. • Heat to 60°C/140°F and then set aside to cool. • Store, covered, at room temperature for at least 5 days before using.	• 1 coconut apple • 2 cloves black garlic • pickled turnip, sliced • pickled radish, sliced • 30 g wakame seaweed • 20 g codium seaweed • sea salt • cumaru vinaigrette in which the turnip was marinated
Seaweed powder	• 20 g codium seaweed • 10 g nori seaweed • 10 g wakame seeweed	• Preheat the oven to 60 °C/140°F. • Spread the codium seaweed in a single layer on a baking sheet and bake for 12 hours. • Remove from oven and cool. • In a blender, combine the 3 seaweeds thoroughly. • Pass through a fine sieve (strainer), then place in a covered container and set aside.	• Peel the coconut apple, open, remove the pulp and set aside. • Peel the garlic cloves then mash them with a fork to make a purée. Add a little vanilla oil and set aside.
Pickled turnip and radish	• 75 g turnip snowball, peeled • 150 ml white wine vinegar • 40 g sugar • 8 g salt • 6 cumaru seeds • 75 g radish	• In a medium pan place 75 ml vinegar, 20 g sugar, 4 g salt, and 3 cumaru seeds. Place over low heat, stirring occasionally until the sugar and salt have dissolved. Do not allow to boil. • Remove from the heat, transfer the liquid to a bowl and add the turnip. • When cool place in the refrigerator. • Repeat the same process with the radish.	• On a plate, place a spoonful of the coconut apple and sprinkle some seaweed powder over it. • Arrange some slices of the pickled turnip and radish alongside the coconut apple. • In the centre place a little mashed black garlic, and some fronds of the wakame and codium seaweed. • Finish with a sprinkling of sea salt, a drop of vanilla oil and a drizzle of the cumaru vinaigrette in which the turnip was pickled.

Cashew

Every time that I host a foreign chef, I amuse myself showing them a cashew in natura. I tell them that the nut is, in fact, the fruit. And that this fruit, when it is still on the tree, comes with a peduncle, which we call caju, or cashew. It is fun showing people this peduncle's flavor and aroma, its juice, the caipirinha we prepare with it, its possibilities in the kitchen. Even more fun is getting a foreign person to see them both together, the peduncle shape, colour, beauty, aroma and the strangeness of seeing a fruit dangling from it.

The cashew peduncle, or apple, is also used to make *cajuína*, a popular drink in northeast Brazil. I use *cajuína* in the recipe for Cajuína, prawn, chayote, pickled onion and tamarind reduction on page 270 of this book.

Cashew nut, in its natural shape, has different moments and different culinary applications. While still unripe, before its peduncle has been wholly formed, the fruit is called mature, and may be cooked and eaten, with flavor notes and texture very different from the cashew nut that everyone knows. The ripe peduncle leaves the fruit – or the nut – at the right stage of maturity, but it is still enclosed in a green, hard shell, which must be toasted and broken for one to find the actual nut.

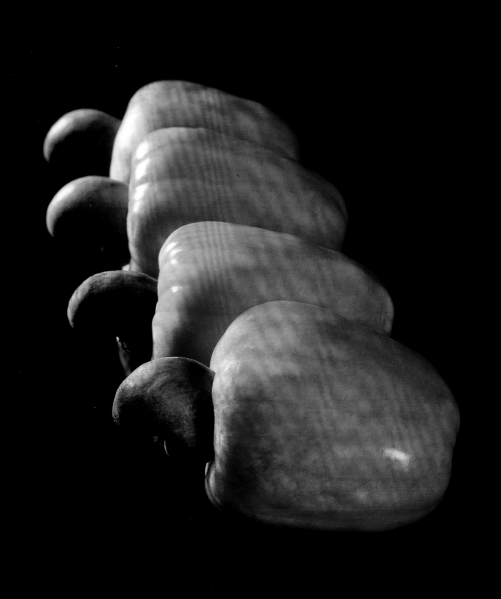

Cajuína, prawn, pickled chayote, onion and tamarind purée

SERVES 4

	Ingredients	Preparation
Pickled chayote	• 150 g chayote • 5 g salt • 150 g white wine vinegar	• Using a mandoline, cut the chayote very thinly into 1-mm slices. • Place the the salt and vinegar in a bowl with 50 ml of water. Mix well together and add the sliced chayote. • Cover and set aside in the refrigerator for a week.
Tamarind purée	• 500 g pulp of tamarind • 80 g sugar	• Place the tamarind and the sugar in a medium pan. Cook over low heat stirring occasionally until reduced to the consistency of a syrup. • Cover and, when cold, set aside in the refrigerator.
Cajuína	• 500 ml cajuína (see page 268) • 35 g yuzu	• Mix the cajuína and yuzu and set aside in the refrigerator. • A couple of minutes before serving place in the freezer; it should be served very cold.
Prawns	• 8 medium prawns (shrimp), peeled and deveined	• Have ready a large bowl of water with plenty of ice. • Bring a large pan of salted water to the boil and blanch the prawns (shrimp) for about 45 seconds. • Strain the prawns and place immediately in the bowl of iced water. • When quite cold, strain and set aside.

Finish and Presentation

• 4 pearl onions, peeled and cut in half
• 12 chive leaves, cut into 5-cm lengths
• coriander (cilantro) sprouts

• Chill 4 deep serving dishes.
• Pre-heat a dry frying pan or skillet and toast the pearl onion halves.
• When nicely coloured remove the onions from the pan, separate the petals and set aside.
• Cut the pickled chayote into tiny pieces, 0.5 cm x 3 cm.
• In the bottom of a chilled deep dish, place a small heap of chopped chives and coriander (cilantro) sprouts.
• Place two prawns (shrimp) on top of the herbs.
• Add the pickled chayote.
• Drop some of the tamarind reduction into the concave onion petals and arrange on the dish.
• Finish by drizzling 2 spoonfuls of the cold cajuína over the whole dish and serve immediately.

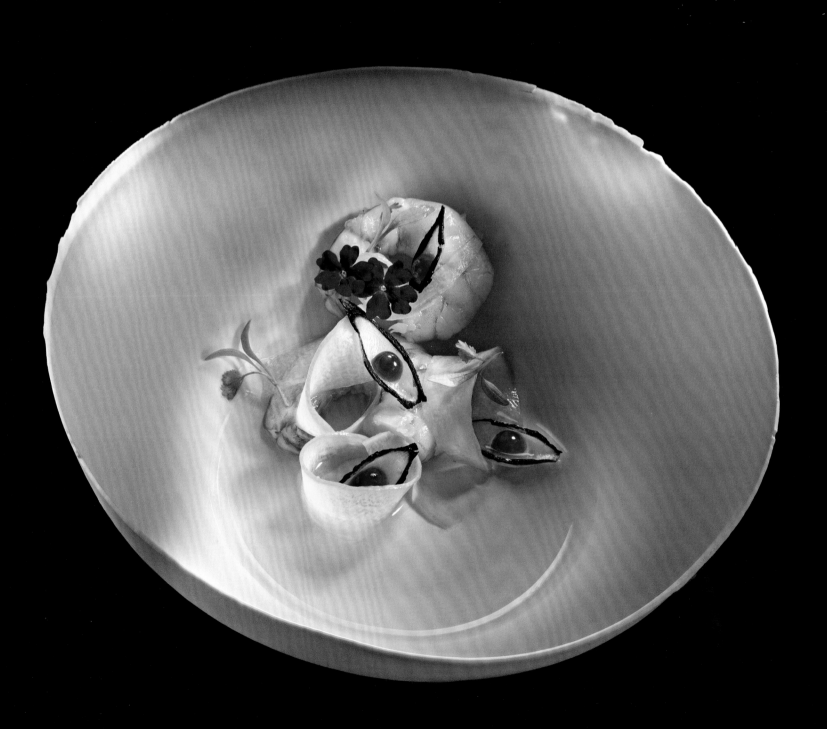

Brazil nut

Brazil nuts are among the most well-known of Amazonian produce. Their popularity has ensured that they aren't as endangered as some other Brazilian produce, but numbers of brazil nut trees have still dwindled as a result of deforestation.

Because of their majestic height, brazil nut trees are easy to find in the forest. The ancient trees dominate the skyline and tower over the canopy. Cutting down the trees is now illegal in Brazil. This was an important measure, but only a small step towards controlling the rate of deforestation in the country. Today, the rate of deforestation has dropped, but is still far from ideal.

Though called a nut, the brazil nut is actually a seed and it grows inside a hard fruit resembling a coconut. Only two animals are able to break through the shell of this fruit and eat the brazil nuts: monkeys, who pick the coconuts and throw them from the trees on to the ground, making them break with the fall, and *cotias* or *agouty*, common Amazonian rodents.

Lightly toasted black rice with green vegetables and brazil nuts

SERVES 4

	Ingredients	Preparation	Finish and Presentation
Brazil nut milk	• **100 g brazil nuts** • **salt**	• Place the Brazil nuts in a blender with 300 ml water and process until smooth. • Strain through a fine chinois. • Season with a little salt and set aside.	• Place a serving of the black rice in the middle of a flat dish. • Drain the celery and spring onion strips thoroughly and arrange over the rice • Arrange pieces of the toasted vegetables over the rice. • Pour the brazil nut milk around the rice.
Black rice	• **50 ml olive oil, plus extra for frying** • **50 g minced onion** • **200 g black rice** • **100 ml white wine** • **1 litre vegetable stock** • **1 g saffron** • **5 g minced garlic** • **salt and pepper**	• Place the olive oil in a medium pan, add the onion, cover and sweat over low heat until soft. • Add the rice and the white wine and simmer until the wine has been absorbed. • Add the vegetable stock gradually and then the saffron and cook for about 30 minutes over medium heat or until the rice is al dente. • Place a little olive oil in a frying pan or skillet over fairly high heat, add the garlic and sauté. • Add the rice and fry until crispy. Set aside to keep warm.	
Green vegetables	• **50 g spring onions (scallions)** • **50 g celery** • **100 g leek, white part only, carefully rinsed** • **1 green bell pepper** • **8 stalks asparagus** • **100 g snow peas** • **olive oil, for toasting and frying** • **100 g broccoli**	• Slice the spring onions (scallions) down the middle then slice it crosswise into 0.2-mm pieces. • Using a mandoline slice the celery into pieces approximately 0.2 mm thick. • Place the celery slices into a bowl of water and ice so that they curl slightly. • Cut the leek into 5-cm rounds, then cut in half crosswise. • Cut the green bell pepper into strips, then cut diagonally one way and then the other to make diamond shapes. • Clean the asparagus, trim the ends, then cut into 5-cm lengths. • Slice the snow peas diagonally crosswise in 1-cm strips. • Heat a pan over medium heat, add a little olive oil and lightly toast the leek, green bell pepper, asparagus and the snow peas. Set aside and keep warm. • Separate the broccoli into florets and wash thoroughly in clean water. • Bring a large pan of water to the boil and blanch the broccoli florets, then drain. • Heat a little olive oil in a frying pan or skillet over high heat, and sauté the broccoli. Set aside and keep warm.	

Brazil nut macaron

SERVES 4

	Ingredients	Preparation
Brazil nut flour	• 250 g shelled brazil nuts • 250 g icing (confectioners') sugar • 60 g cornflour (corn starch)	• Process all of the ingredients in a food processor until you have a fine powder. • Sift the powder and set aside.
Macaron	• 250 g brazil nut flour (above) • 100 g egg white • 170 g caster (superfine) sugar • 100 g natural yogurt	• Preheat the oven to 150°C/300°F and line a baking sheet with baking parchment. • Suspend a heatproof bowl over a pan of simmering water and add the egg whites and caster sugar. Stir over the heat until the sugar has dissolved. • Transfer the mixture to the bowl of a stand mixer and whisk to form a stiff meringue. • Carefully fold in the brazil nut flour until thoroughly combined. • Transfer the meringue to a piping bag and pipe 1½ in/4 cm circles onto the prepared baking sheet. • Bake in the preheated oven for 12 minutes. • Once cool, remove for the baking parchment and fill with natural yogurt.

Caramelized brazil nuts

SERVES 4

Caramelized brazil nuts

Ingredients

- 125 g brazil nuts, shelled
- 45 g caster (superfine) sugar
- 11 g water
- 7.5 g unsalted butter, cold
- 100 g 70% cocoa dark chocolate
- 3 tablespoons cocoa powder

Preparation

- Cut the brazil nuts in half and set aside.
- Heat the sugar with 11 ml of water in a small pan over medium heat until it reaches 117°C/243°F and a syrup has formed.
- Add the nuts to the pan and caramelized them in the syrup.
- Melt the chocolate over a bain marie.
- Add the nuts to the chocolate and mix to coat.
- Transfer the chocolate-covered nuts to a cooling rack and leave to set.
- Place the cocoa powder in a bowl and roll the nuts through to coat. Set aside until ready to serve.

Honey

Since 1934 Brazilian law has decreed that only melliferous secretion with a water content of 20 per cent or less, from African or European bees introduced into the country, can be called, and sold as, honey. This legislation unintentionally delivered a silent blow against the Brazilian ecosystem. There are many species of bee native to Brazil which produce a honey with too high a water content to conform to this requirement. But it has incredible organoleptic qualities, which are uncommon in honey, and very significant medicinal properties. It is still sold, therefore, because people value its health-giving properties, but only as an unauthorized and therefore marginal product, sold below its cost. Recently I set up an organization whose first battle will be to press for a change in the legislation, so that this product can be extracted and sold legally on the open market for a fair price. Our native bees need healthy, balanced environments to be able to produce their small quantities of honey and to reproduce. So we need to guarantee that extraction is carried out in the best possible way. If I am successful, I believe that I will achieve economic, cultural and environmental benefits for Brazil.

Red porgy with ariá potatoes and Brazilian honey

SERVES 4

Ingredients

Vinaigrette

- 100 ml lime juice
- 100 ml Brazilian honey
- extra virgin olive oil
- small bunch parsley, finely chopped

Potatoes and red porgy

- 4 ariá potatoes, peeled and cooked
- 4 x 120-g red porgy fillets, skin on

Preparation

- Place the lime juice and the honey in a bowl and whisk well together with enough extra virgin olive oil to make a vinaigrette.
- Mix in the parsley and set aside.

- Cut the potatoes in half and reserve.
- Season the fish with salt and pepper
- Heat a non-stick frying pan or skillet and grill the fish on the skin side only.

Finish and presentation

- **extra virgin olive oil**
- **4 aromatic peppers**
- **salt and pepper**

- Arrange two halves of potato on a plate and pour some honey vinaigrette over them.
- Lay the fish across the potatoes and drizzle some extra virgin olive oil over it.
- Place an aromatic pepper beside the fish.
- Season with salt and pepper and serve.

Nixtamalization

This strange-sounding word describes one of the oldest South-American culinary techniques. Records of this process go back to Incan and Mayan times. The process is very simple, rudimentary even. It consists of immersing a vegetable containing some degree of starch in a solution of water and lime. The reaction between the starch and the alkaline environment makes a crust appear around the vegetable, the thickness of the crust is dependent on the length of the immersion. The famous Mexican tortillas are made out of nixtamalized corn (maize).

This process is followed all over South America, including Brazil. Some of our patisserie has Portuguese roots. This almost always involves high concentrations of sugar – fruits and vegetables conserved in water and sugar syrup. Nixtamalization is, for instance, the basis of one of our most traditional recipes: doce de abobóra, or crystallized pumpkin.

Incredible as it may sound, nixtamalization is now forbidden in Brazil, even though crystallized pumpkin made in this way can be found in some markets. This is one more small controversy where local culture and legislation over food safety come into conflict. Legislators often act on data provided by health and safety authorities. Well, if it doesn't hurt the rest of Latin America, where it isn't illegal, I want to awaken my rebellious side and use the technique. Speaking seriously, I am in favour of experimenting with all techniques, especially when they can take me to places where I could not reach otherwise.

The recipes for Pumpkin, vegetable coal and tapioca ice cream (see page 136) and Green papaya with bacuri snow (see page 236) use this process. It is the only way to achieve almost transparent slices of papaya. And perhaps the contrast between the external crunchiness and internal softness of the crystallized pumpkin justifies following my rebellious side.

Glossary

Glossary

Aerosil

A brand of fumed silica mainly used in the food industry to preserve the qualities of powdered food ingredients. It helps avoid agglomeration in powders and lump formations in liquid and solids mixes. It is also used to stabilize some kind of emulsions or foams.

Agar agar

A gelling agent derived from seaweed, which retains its gelling properties up to a temperature of 80°C/176°F.

Bottarga

The salted and dried roe of the tuna or grey mullet, often used as a garnish.

Brioche flour

An enriched flour used in the making of brioche and other delicate breads.

Cachaça

An alcoholic spirit made from fermented sugarcane juice. A key component of the caipirinha, the national cocktail of Brazil.

Cansanção

A nettle-like plant that must be blanched before eating to neutralize its stinging properties.

Colorau

A red powder derived from dried annatto seeds and used as a food colouring.

Centrifuge

A device that spins at high speeds to separate products into parts based on density.

Chaux vive

See *quicklime*.

Chayote

A green pear-shaped fruit with a dense texture and a mild flavour.

Chinois

A fine-mesh conical sieve (strainer).

Dehydrator

A kitchen appliance that removes the moisture content from food, thereby preserving it and decreasing its volume, and often creating a crunchy texture.

Ice cream stabilizer

A combination of stabilizers and emulsifiers designed to delay ice crystals forming as ice cream freezes. The resulting ice cream has a smoother texture and slower melting time.

Katsuobushi

Dried flakes of skipjack tuna. A common ingredient in Japanese cuisine, most commonly found used in the base of many broths.

Liquid glucose

A thick, syrupy liquid obtained by incomplete hydrolysis of starch and consisting chiefly of dextrose, with dextrins, maltose, and water. Has both medical and culinary applications.

Lactose

A naturally occurring sugar found in milk. It has many culinary applications based on its low sweetness.

Pacojet

A machine used to make sorbets with a very fine texture, as well as other creations such as frozen powders.

Paio sausage

A firm, smoked sausage made from pork loin, garlic, salt and bell pepper. In Brazil, it is commonly used to make *feijoada*.

Quicklime

A widely used chemical compound, also known as calcium oxide. It reacts with several compounds in food to add nutritional and textural properties to different elaborations. In South American cuisine it is used in the process of maize nixtamalization and in the preparation of traditional jams.

Roner

See 'sous vide'.

Rotavapor

A machine used to make sous-vide distillations.

Salamander

A type of grill (broiler) used in professional kitchens, often for browning foods before service.

Sea purslane

A shrub that grows on salt marshes, with salty-tasting leaves.

Silpat

A non-stick silicone baking mat.

Siphon

A utensil originally designed to whip cream and used in modern professional kitchens for the making of foams.

Sous vide

A machine used in professional kitchens to maintain a constant temperature in water. It is used to cook sous-vide for long periods of time at a low and constant temperature. Also known as a Roner.

Thermomix

A food processor that can blend food at different temperatures.

Tonka beans

The fragrant seeds of the cumaru tree. Though bitter to taste, the seeds have an appealing aroma, reminiscent of vanilla and cloves, and are commonly used by the fragrance industry.
In cooking tonka beans are used very sparingly as ingesting large amounts can be toxic.

Transglutaminase

An enzyme used to bond proteins together and to improve the texture of protein-rich foods. In molecular gastronomy it is used to meld new textures with existing tastes.

Vacuum bag

A polyamide bag used for vacuum-sealing food. It is often used by professional kitchens in sous-vide cooking.

Vacuum (thermal) cooker

A cooking device composed of an electric burner that heats a stainless steel pot with very precise temperature control. It also incorporates a vacuum pump that extracts air from the pot, allowing low temperature boiling.

Xantham gum

A product derived from fermented starch, used as a thickening agent and to maintain solids in suspension within a liquid.

Xylitol powder

A powder made out of a naturally occurring sugar substitute found in the fibres of many fruits and vegetables.

Index

CONTENTS

Numbers in italics refer to illustrations

Phaidon Press Limited
Regent's Wharf
All Saints Street
London N1 9PA

Phaidon Press Inc.
180 Varick Street
New York, NY 10014

www.phaidon.com

First published 2013
Reprinted 2013
© 2013 Phaidon Press Limited

ISBN 978 0 7148 6574 4

A CIP catalogue record for this book is available from the British Library

Commissioning Editor: Emilia Terragni
Project Editor: Daniel Hurst
Production Controller: Alenka Oblak

Designed by R2 Design
Recipe and ingredient photographs by Sergio Coimbra
Narrative photographs by Edu Simões

Printed in Italy

The publisher would like to thank Alex Atala for his passion, drive and vision. They would also like to thank Carolina Chagas and Andrea Campos for their hard work and enthusiasm for the project.

Recipe notes

Some of the recipes require advanced techniques, specialist equipment and professional experience to achieve good results.

Exercise a high level of caution when following recipes involving any potentially hazardous activity, including the use of quicklime, high temperatures, open flames and when deep-frying. In particular, when using quicklime and deep-frying add food carefully to avoid splashing, wear long sleeves and gloves, if necessary, to avoid any contact with skin, and never leave unattended.

Cooking times are for guidance only. If using a fan (convection) oven, follow the manufacturer's instructions concerning the oven temperatures.

Some recipes include lightly cooked eggs, meat and fish, and fermented products. These should be avoided by the elderly, infants, pregnant women, convalescents and anyone with an impaired immune system.

Exercise caution when making fermented products, ensuring all equipment is spotlessly clean, and seek expert advice if in any doubt.

Exercise caution and wear protective clothing when undertaking any butchering work.

All herbs, shoots, flowers, berries, seeds and vegetables should be picked fresh from a clean source. Exercise caution when foraging for ingredients. Any foraged ingredients should only be eaten if an expert has deemed them safe to eat.

When no quantity is specified, for example of oils, salts and herbs used for finishing dishes, quantities are discretionary and flexible.